W9-DFS-495

SCHOOLCRAFT
COLLEGE LIBRARY

HANNELORE SACHS

THE RENAISSANCE WOMAN

McGRAW-HILL
Book Company
NEW YORK

Translated from the German by Marianne Herzfeld,
revised by Professor D. Talbot Rice
We also want to thank Miss M. V. Downie for her assistance

HQ
1148
.S213

Copyright 1971 by Edition Leipzig
Library of Congress Catalog Card No. 79 154549
McGraw-Hill Code No. 07-054375-5
Printed in the German Democratic Republic

CONTENTS

Introduction   7

Upbringing and Education of Young Girls   14

Matrimony, Motherhood and Domestic Life   20

Physical Culture and Cosmetics—Fashion and
Jewelry   28

The Practice of Art   36

Work and Public Activities   41

Women Slaves, Beggars, Witches, Courtesans
and Concubines   49

Comments on the Pictures   54

Bibliography   60

Sources of Illustrations   62

Plates

INTRODUCTION

Ever since Jakob Burckhardt described *Die Kultur der Renaissance in Italien* the picture of the cultivated and emancipated woman has dominated the concept of a woman's life of that time. Glorified in literature, art and history, the proud and self-confident ladies of the Florentine aristocracy and of the nobility of northern Italy have been known, almost as well as the men of their circles, as the embodiment of the marked individuality of the Renaissance. Compared with them, the women in the countries north of the Alps are shown by their numerous extant portraits as plain burgher women, their activities evidently being limited to household and family life. Both types represent the image of woman of that period. They are typical of mankind at the beginning of modern times. Their extreme dissimilarity, conditioned by social and regional differences, indicates the wide variation between the several types of the Renaissance woman.

The present study will deal mainly with the women in the most economically advanced countries of Europe—Germany, the Netherlands, England and France, as well as with those in Italy, although in the latter country an economic regression could already be noted at the turn of the 15th century; this, however, had not yet affected the dominant role of Italian culture among neighbouring countries. Other countries will, however, also be mentioned if influenced by the culture of the Renaissance insofar as any special aspects of the life of women are known.

Most of the space will be devoted to the women of the ruling classes, that is of patricians, the lower and higher ranks of the nobility and the princely families, as it is their lives which underwent the greatest change since the middle ages and wherein the influence of Renaissance culture was most far-reaching. It is there that we have the most ample documentary material from pictorial and literary sources. More scanty are the records of the specific conditions governing the life of the peasant women and of the women among the underprivileged townspeople. It is evident, however, that their social position contrasted with the image of the woman of the Renaissance, as pictured by Burckhardt; his description is biased and calls for some criticism. Even within the bourgeoisie, which at that time was becoming more and more influential in the fields of culture and economy, there were considerable differences ranging from the artisans and retail dealers, whose wives were their helpmates, to the entrepreneurs, merchants and bankers with seignorial households. The degrees of the scale were characterized by notable divergencies in education, in costume, in the physical culture of women, in fact, by their whole way of life.

The basis of the culture of the 16th century was the new mode of production characteristic of early capitalism, expanding from the Italian cities and the Netherlands to large parts of Europe. The simple commodity production known in feudal times was suppressed step by step; the first manufactories were established, and with them came the new class of wage earners, who had to sell their labour power to employers. Trade expanded across national frontiers, even beyond Europe to the then recently discovered regions overseas. Banking too was highly developed, money transactions and the exploitation of mining proved to be the most profitable sources of income for the big trading houses. All this process was in the hands of the burghers in the towns.

Consistent with this new economic development was the fundamental change in mental attitude in the 15th and 16th centuries. Humanism broke down the narrow barriers of mediaeval thought, which had been dominated by the tenets of the Church. Taking the ancients as models, humanism asked for men of all-embracing culture. Science made rapid progress. Inventions in all fields of technical skill and the discovery of far-away countries and continents broadened the view of life. Men proudly became conscious of their achievements and their successes. The era of the early bourgeois revolution had resulted not only in a revival of classical antiquity but also in a "rebirth of man," who was trying to master nature and determine his own destiny. As Friedrich Engels stated, it was that splendid epoch in the history of mankind that brought forth giants in thought, passion and character and which was the starting point for the civilization of modern times.

In a restricted manner, this new self-confidence became noticeable also in the attitude and life of women. Many of them became personalities, known to history; they were outstanding through their political activities and the part they played in the spheres of knowledge and art. This was founded on an adequate education and erudition which gave scope for the expansion of their abilities. The Humanists included women in their pedagogical theories and educational programmes; they wanted women to take an interest in the humanities so as to become congenial partners, with intellects equal to that of the men. In fact, however, these theories influenced only a very small part of the female population. They were chiefly limited to those women who were educated by the Humanists themselves and grew up and lived in a select atmosphere open to the advance of art and knowledge. This applied specifically to the small courts of northern Italy: Ferrara, Mantua, Urbino. There the education enjoyed by the daughters of the princes and nobles already included in the 15th century not only the elementary subjects, the specially feminine accomplishments and the rules of social conduct, but also a basic knowledge of the humanities through the study of Latin and the authors of antiquity. To this were added the entertainments usual at these courts, where the young ladies met highly cultivated men, thereby widening their own outlook. These were the circumstances under which those noblewomen grew up, later to acquire fame as the brilliant centres of the literary and philosophical circles of their courts. Interest has again and again been focused on them alone and thereby has helped to form a much too one-sided image of the woman of the Renaissance.

Starting from Italy humanism expanded in the 16th century to the courts of Spain, France and England and met there with a considerable amount of encouragement. At these courts there were also several women prominent through their sound humanistic knowledge and literary activities. But again it was only members of the reigning houses and the nobility who proved eager to dedicate themselves to the study of Plato while, with few exceptions, the female members of the bourgeoisie were unable to share in this culture or in any refined intellectual activities. In Germany the education of young girls, even in the ranks of the nobility, was restricted to needlework and religion; no example can be cited comparable to such shining personalities as Isabella d'Este or Margaret of Navarre. Only the Humanists taught their own children Latin, and in the convents there were a few women occupied with the study of some branches of knowledge; but the majority of women enjoyed no education other than a modicum of reading and writing. Kitchen and house, the mother's and housewife's role, manual work from morning to night, remained their domain. The ideal of the respectable wife, faithfully caring for her family and home, was prevalent particularly in the Protestant north; pious, humble and unassuming

8

she had to submit to her husband, to bring up her children and to limit her activities almost exclusively to the family. Erudition was all but taboo for her. This kind of life formed the rule for the greater part of the female population in all European countries.

Even in Italy where, at least at the courts and in the houses of the leading families, the intellectual equality of the sexes was acknowledged, there was no question of any legal equality. The very rights of the woman with regard to her husband were narrowly circumscribed by law. There were a few champions of equal rights for the sexes, but their demands remained purely theoretical. They show, however, to what prohibitions and restrictions in their public activities even the women of the advanced society of a city state like Florence had to submit. Women were for instance not entitled to occupy any public office, could not adopt children, go bail for any body, act as guardian or representative of any person of minor age, except of their own children, and even for these they were not allowed to appoint a guardian (34). Only in business was equality secured for them by the fast growth of trade in the days of early capitalism.

In private life the right to lead and to make decisions devolved without any question upon a male member of the family, whether father, husband or son. Family life was regulated in a patriarchal way, although the wife was sometimes granted independence in economic matters relating to the household; in kitchen and house, the sphere most particularly her own, she could govern and show her practical abilities. But for the outward world the husband was the representative of his wife, as was the father of his still unmarried daughters and, after his death, their guardian or their brothers were responsible for them. As in the middle ages, the unmarried women of the nobility as well as those of the bourgeoisie found refuge and were cared for in convents.

Although most women continued to live in the traditional manner within the family circle, social and economic conditions gave rise to new outlooks, contrasting with those of the middle ages. This applies in particular to the burghers in the towns, to whom the prosperity of commerce and the trades had procured the financial base for greater daily expenditures. Luxurious clothing was at that time enjoyed by both men and women, and by the burghers as well as by the nobility; it made itself felt even among the peasants. To this was added a profusion of jewelry and of objects of artistic handicraft,

which all served to show off the owner's prosperity. An extensive foreign trade enriched the markets by the importation of goods and spread especially the luxury goods from the Far East over all parts of Europe. Within the reach of women there now came a variety of cosmetics, make-up, ointments and perfumes. These were made first in Italy but before long in all other countries of Europe as well. Numerous anti-luxury decrees were issued to stop excesses. A permissible maximum expenditure for clothing and jewelry was prescribed for each social rank, together with a regulation for the appropriate length of any festivities.

The differences in the life of the women were determined by the strict division of the population into three main classes: the peasants, the burghers and the nobles and, furthermore, the sub-classification of the townspeople into patricians, artisans, petty tradesmen and wage earners; among these there were still other social gradations. The boundaries of the social ranks made themselves felt more than those separating countries. Although the women in each of the European countries differed from those in the others as to clothes, headdress and customs, in the 16th century the way a patrician woman of Nuremberg spent her days probably resembled closely that of the merchant's wife in Amsterdam, Lübeck, Lyon, Cracow or Florence. It was, however, unlike that of the artisan's wife in any of these towns and still very different from the hard-working day of the peasant woman in the country or from that spent in luxury by the noblewomen in their castles.

Common to all women was the duty of running the household. This involved at that time much more work than nowadays, as with the upbringing of the children, who were numerous in each family. In the well-to-do classes the housewife usually had several maids to help her, so that she had only to control the cooking, roasting and baking, and could find time for fine needlework. For the artisan's wife there was, in addition to the activities in kitchen and house, the works she had to do for her husband's trade, chiefly selling the goods; and the peasant woman had, as at all times, to take her share in work in the fields and stables.

Our concept of life in the Renaissance is based on many literary sources and works of art. These transmit to us pictures of the life at that period in a realistic as well as in an idealized form. Rich, however, as this material is, it shows significant deficiencies, especially with regard

9

to everyday life, for contemporaries always consider it beneath their dignity to record it, and that the unusual alone is worth their notice. Even travellers, as a rule, register only customs at variance with those of their home, and historians restrict their reports to public life. Unlike these sources it is the personal papers, diaries and letters, which provide the best information and an often quite casual but detailed insight into the traditions and ways of daily life. A large number of such documents is extant from the Renaissance. The letters written by the educated women reveal what aroused their interest or constituted problems for them. They record the rules laid down for the use of cosmetics, recipes for make-up and perfumes, describe travels and festivities, the worries occasioned by their servants, the marriage of sons and daughters and the dowry provided for them. Carefully kept diaries of merchants put on record the cost of the dowry, of the gifts for the bride, and the outlay for the wedding festivities as well as other household expenses. The information given by these individual examples is supplemented by the numerous regulations and decrees which enable us to reconstruct the rites prevailing at weddings and other festivities, the conditions existing in schools, the ways of jurisdiction and many other events forming part of the women's existence.

Finally there are a great many treatises and theories describing the ideal concept at that epoch of the woman's life and looks. The Humanists of the Early Renaissance had written about the education of young girls and defined their concept of family life. The treatises of the 16th century analyzed chiefly the woman's beauty and the means of preserving and enhancing it. Agnolo Firenzuola, 1493–1548, a monk and lawyer at the papal Curia, formulated a downright canon of female beauty, stating the ideal shape of the individual parts of the body, the colours most desirable for the hair, the eyebrows, lips and cheeks, which should combine to create the perfect harmony of the woman's appearance. According to him and to the general taste of the period, the hair must be long, thick and fair, of a soft yellow, turning brown; the skin, light and clear, but not pale; the eyes dark brown, large and somewhat vaulted, their sclera shimmering blue. The nose ought not to be curved, as aquiline noses do not suit women; the mouth should be small, the lips round, the chin round with a dimple; the neck rounded and fairly long, the Adam's apple not protruding. Broad shoulders and prominent breasts were thought to add to the woman's beauty, and her hands ought to be white, soft and rounded, her legs long and her feet small.

The Female Servants of Artisans, of Burghers and of Peasants

At the same time Heinrich Bebel, a popular writer in Germany, at that time, declared that the perfectly beautiful woman ought to possess three times seven bodily charms; later he even increased this number to thirty.

In contrast to the attention paid to the physical charms of the woman by the Renaissance, the Reformation stressed the merit of her moral qualities. The *Ehezuchtbüchlein* (Little Manual of Correct Behaviour in Matrimony) by Johann Fischart, 1578, stipulated that the wife had to be the "friendly and obedient lifelong partner of her husband, soothing, and forming his complement." Martin Luther says in his *Lob eines frommen Weibes* (Praise of a Pious Wife): "A pious, God-fearing wife is a rare treasure, more noble and precious than a pearl. Her husband relies on her and trusts her in every respect. She gives him joy and makes him happy, does not distress him, shows loving kindness to him all through his life, and never gives him pain. She handles flax and wool, likes to work with her hands; she benefits the house and resembles the merchant's ship which brings many goods from far-away countries. She rises early, feeds her servants and gives to the maids what is their due. She likes working and caring for what concerns her and does not busy herself with what is not her concern. She girds her loins and stretches her arms, works with energy in the house. She notices what is convenient and prevents damage. Her light is not extinguished at night. She puts her hand to the distaff and her fingers grip the spindle, she works with pleasure and diligence. She holds her hands over the poor and needy."

Assurance and ease in social behaviour, the mastery of manners were the chief requirements of all women of high rank. There were, therefore, scores of books treating of the education of young girls and of the manners of women (37). Together with devotional literature, manuals of manners formed the largest part of all printed matter in the 16th century. The chief work was the *Cortegiano* by Count Baldassare Castiglione, published for the first time in 1528. It formed the basis for all similar books, was translated into many languages and extended its influence far outside the boundaries of Italy. It describes the perfect courtier and supplements his picture by that of the perfect lady. She should be as beautiful as she was sensible and cultured, must take an interest in arts and letters, and be able to act as hostess and to entertain. It was thought to be the main duty of women to establish perfect harmony between their beauty, their words and the grace of their movements. The prototype of this ideal were the ladies among whom Castiglione lived at the courts of the Italian princes, and whose praise was sung by the poets in many a verse.

In addition to the example given in literature there are the representations of women in all branches of art, painting, drawing and sculpture. The large number of portraits of women, but also genre pictures, as well as religious and mythological scenes impart a fair knowledge of their appearance, their activities and their environment. In the 15th and 16th centuries religious subjects still prevailed in art. Many altars were dedicated and pictures painted for churches and for domestic devotion, showing the Virgin, Bible stories and legends of saints—most of them against a contemporary background. The saints were dressed according to the fashion of the Renaissance. The events took place in a definite existing landscape or town, in surroundings which minutely reproduced the world in which the contemporary observer lived. Frequently portraits of the donors or of members of their family were inserted as spectators or as figures taking part in the scene represented.

In the middle ages the Virgin was shown in idealized beauty as the unapproachable Queen of Heaven, but in the pictures of the Renaissance the contemporary type of woman is so clearly evidenced that one fancies that young patrician women with their children must have sat as models.

The general fondness for detail in biblical stories and in legends offered the opportunity to depict everyday life and events which had otherwise been neglected in art. Pictures of the birth of Mary or St. John led the spectator to a lying-in room in a burgher's house. Those of the wedding at Cana or of Christ visiting Mary and Martha allow an insight into the contemporary kitchen. Moreover, in the Early Italian Renaissance there were for the first time representations of classical themes which, also transferred to the 15th century, reflected the customs of that epoch.

The practice of lovingly describing the background of religious or mythological scenes persisted until the time of the High Renaissance in Italy. Then, however, the divine figures were set in a higher region, transfigured and idealized, and thereby removed from the earthly sphere. Yet even in these images of the Virgin or of saints the contemporary ideal of the female personality can be detected, the harmony of body and mind, of dignity and charm. Even had the works of Christian art alone survived from these two centuries we should still have some knowledge of the appearance of the woman of the Renaissance and of the changes her type underwent due to fashion and taste.

But there are extant also large numbers of portraits, the authentic likenesses of individual women of all circles and every age. The new longing for asserting oneself, the new self-confidence had made portraiture the chief theme of secular art. People had their portraits made so that their individual features might be faithfully retained and simultaneously to prove their social rank by their garments and jewelry.

It must be stated, however, that at the beginning of this art in modern times the female portrait was inferior to the male's, as the artists retained the mediaeval idealization longer in the female portraits. In the portraits of donors those of the women are still generalized, showing them with the high, curved forehead and the small mouth of characteristic Gothic pictures of the Virgin, whereas the men are already characterized as individuals. The first women portrayed as individuals with faithfully reproduced features appear in the art of the Netherlands of the early 15th century. The Netherlandish merchants and their Italian partners had single and double portraits made of themselves and their wives. In the images of these burgher women from the Netherlands that survive, the details of their features and their costumes are very exact, in particular their ingeniously draped bonnets as, for instance, in the paintings of Jan van Eyck, Rogier van der Weyden and of the Master of Flémalle.

Since approximately 1440, medals were stamped in Italy, for which the coins of the Roman emperors were taken as prototypes; they showed on one side the profile portrait of the patron, on the other an allegory bearing some relation to his life. They were used as personal gifts and memorials in order to assure personal fame and so to achieve immortality. Many women of patrician rank and of the nobility tried to immortalize themselves by these means. At the same time portraits of women were first painted, though to begin with, preference was given to purely profile views such as are usual for medals. At the beginning of the century, the ladies of the nobility, still dressed in the imaginative fashion of the court of Burgundy, stood in the foreground of the paintings; the daughters of the patriciate of the towns took them as

their models. Embellished by their artistic coiffures, in their sumptuous clothes, they appeared more self-confident and more open-minded than their homely sisters in the northern countries.

During the Early Italian Renaissance portrait busts of marble or clay were more popular even than the painted portraits. Like those of the Roman Republican era, they showed the individual who was portrayed plain and unaffected by any idealization. There are several busts of young girls among them. Probably they were made when the daughters were married and left the family house so that the parents might retain the portrait as a memorial of their child. The portraits of these self-assured, rather dashing young ladies are of such a lively immediacy that one could take them for photographic snapshots.

Since the High Renaissance the importance of the painted portrait has surpassed that of the bust. Portraits were greatly varied, including the most diverse views and sections of views. The half- or three-quarters length representations of the noble and princely ladies stressed their dignity. Simultaneously the most subtle psychological shading and a greater emphasis on the portrayed person's mentality became noticeable. Yet an idealization tending to show the coveted, youthfully smooth beauty was characteristic of many portraits of ladies. Nevertheless an elderly, poor and plain woman was also deemed worthy of portrayal by Giorgione, the master painter of Venice's feminine beauty. (Ill. 11)

German paintings of the 16th century show innumerable variants of the portraits of the more simple burgher women. With their traditional bonnets and their high-necked dresses they clearly represent the ideal of the respectable, virtuous and pious housewife and mother. Naively enjoying their property, these women put on their Sunday best and all their jewelry when sitting for their portraits, and the artists complied with their wishes and reproduced every single detail in the most subtle way. Frequently—in particular in the Netherlandish art—the woman portrayed is shown in action in one way or another, making music, reading a book or writing a letter, thereby stressing her higher education.

In the democratically minded Netherlands, wholly secular themes gained ground early on. Everyday life and the world surrounding it now appeared worthy of representation, and in the mid-sixteenth century some artists began to specialize in new branches of secular art, such as still life, portraiture or genre pictures. Pieter Brueghel watched the peasants at their work and at rowdy festivities, village weddings, country fairs, carnival processions. He depicted the crowd in towns and villages, and put on record the types of the woman beggar and the peasant woman. Pieter Aartsen and Joachim Beuckelaer turned their attention to markets and kitchens; the market woman selling her wares, the maids at their work, the cook at the kitchen range, they all are shown either as large single figures or forming part of a kind of still life. Mythological subjects too frequently offered opportunities to show women at work.

Still more often did printed graphic works describe customs and usages, focus a critical light upon social conditions, and even pillory these.

Pamphlets with woodcuts of unmistakable meaning and those with explanatory texts made widely known the complaints by maids about their hard work, caricatured adultery and matrimonial quarrels or, in the service of the reformatory propaganda, reviled the behaviour of monks and nuns. Drawings, woodcuts and etchings in black and white have handed down to us pictures of public events, otf he generally prevalent burning of witches, and also of intimate domestic life such as the woman's bath or the nursing of a child.

The female nude, the ideal of woman's beauty, was personified by the goddesses of ancient mythology. The image of Venus, of Diana, but also of Cleopatra, Lucretia, the Three Graces and of many other women from legend or history had been made known, had even been made popular by humanism. They formed the models for the many variants of representations of female beauty in painting and sculpture. One might study in them the dissimilarity of female beauty as it was conceived by the different countries, as well as by changes of taste.

The ideal of the Early Italian Renaissance was the young girl, hardly yet developed, slim and sometimes with an almost austere beauty, as we find it in the Graces and goddesses of Botticelli. The High Renaissance preferred ripe and voluptuous beauty with well-rounded outlines as shown in pictures of Venus by the Venetian masters of the 16th century. The art of the Netherlands, opposed to this idealization, preferred realistic images of the nude seen by sober-minded artists. In Germany Dürer tried to establish a canon of proportions which was based on what he had learned in the course of his study of nature, while Lucas Cranach's over-slim ladies in his pictures of Venus suited the taste of the court of the Elector of Saxony at Wittenberg.

UPBRINGING AND EDUCATION OF YOUNG GIRLS

In all European countries education had been considerably changed and improved in the 16th century under the influence of humanism. In the forefront stood the studies reserved for boys, but in the education of girls, too, innovations were introduced to what had been usual in the middle ages. Schools for girls were established everywhere to teach the fundamentals of reading and writing which became common knowledge at least in the towns. In their pedagogical theories the Humanists even provided for equality in the teaching of all branches of knowledge for boys and girls. In reality, however, their theories did not benefit many members of the female sex, though among these were some personalities who stood out because of their quite exceptional culture and talent. In the 16th century the participation of women in art and knowledge reached heights which were not surpassed until the 19th century.

This development of women's faculties was founded on a new appreciation of their personalities which asserted itself first in Italy, parallel with the expansion of humanism. The Humanists demanded that the principle *mulier taceat in ecclesia*, upheld by the mediaeval Church, be given up and that women be acknowledged as individual personalities intellectually equal with men; they had therefore to be given an adequate education. As early as the 15th century the theoretical writings of Bruni and Alberti had contained the first allusions to the education of young girls; while the mediaeval methods of education had mainly stressed the necessity of "guarding" them and of bringing them up to be modest and chaste, humble and quiet, now the training of the women's intellect was required in order to make them partners of intellectual equality with their husbands and to enable them to teach their children the rudiments of knowledge. According to the Humanists all women of the cultured classes should prove themselves worthy of their famous prototypes in antiquity and form their minds by the study of knowledge and science (Bruni). Besides reading and writing they were therefore asked to master Latin, to be able not only to read and study the Fathers of the Church, but also the literature of the ancients and the classical writings on philosophy and history. Various guides which recommended the authors to be chosen were published for the intellectual activities of women. According to the general educational aims of the Humanists, the studies of women ought to include not only literature, but also geometry, arithmetic and astrology. There were even

14

detailed instructions in prosody, since the educated woman was supposed to be able to express her thoughts and emotions in Latin verse.

These theoretical demands soon showed results. Well-known Humanists were entertained at the courts to impart the coveted cultural ideal to the children, and there the young girls too received a comprehensive humanistic education. It became a matter of course for young ladies of rank to master Latin and to know the writers of antiquity. Pietro Bembo, the Humanist and poet, highly esteemed at the courts of northern Italy in the early 16th century, even said: "A young girl ought to learn Latin as this greatly enhances her charm." Familiarity with Greek was usually reserved for boys, but some instances of girls learning it are known. Outstanding among these was Caecilia Gonzaga who, according to a letter dated 1435, boasted an admirable fluency in Greek already at the age often; she was taught by Vittorino da Feltre, a Humanist much interested in educational problems. More often, however, mention is made of young girls who greeted exalted personalities with Latin speeches, composed by themselves: the eleven-year-old Margherita Solari is said to have thus welcomed King Charles VIII of France, Battista de Montefeltre the Emperor Sigismund and Pope Martin V, and Battista Sforza Pope Pius II.

This high cultural level made the young noblewomen equal partners in conversation with Humanists, poets and artists, and quite often it was a woman who formed the centre of their social circle. The best-known instance of this is Isabella d'Este, the wife of the Margrave of Mantua, who owed her renown as *prima donna del mondo* not alone to her beauty and her good taste in questions of fashion, but mainly to her fame as a brilliant woman, taking interest in all branches of art and knowledge. She and her brothers and sisters were given in their childhood a befitting education at the art-loving court of Ferrara; it included, together with the cultivation of social manners and of artistic and practical skills, the rudiments of Latin. While her sister Beatrice later concerned herself only with riding and social entertainments, Isabella eagerly followed up her studies after her marriage, though the Margrave was keener on leading an active life, on hunting and waging war. She engaged teachers for her Latin studies and is said to have written Latin exercises in composition and made translations still at the age of forty. She read Virgil, Ovid, Horace and Catullus just as well as contemporary literature. Her library was comprehensive, as she showed the same passion in assembling it as for her collection of works of art; her interest embraced alike poetry, history, philosophy and art. She maintained all through her life an extensive correspondence with the most famous men and women of her time and was always surrounded by a circle of artists and scholars at her home in the castle of Mantua. So Lorenzo Costa's allegorical painting with Isabella as crowned centre of an Arcadian court of the Muses does not lack a certain foundation in reality. (Ill. 75)

Nor was the education of women inferior at other Italian courts. Veronica de Gambara, the gifted and talented ruler of Correggio, was known for her poetry. In Urbino Battista Sforza, wife of Federico da Montefeltre, aroused the admiration of her contemporaries by her knowledge of Greek, her Latin speeches and her exceptional memory. Urbino remained a centre of intellectual life in the following generation, thanks to the unusual erudition and the outstanding personality of Elisabetta Gonzaga. Like the spirited Emilia Pia with her sceptical and ironical wit, she too was one of the much admired interlocutors of Baldassare Castiglione, quoted by him as a model for the perfect lady in his *Cortegiano*, when he stipulated that, notwithstanding their higher education, women ought to retain a *dolcezza femminile* as a specially feminine quality: charm, beauty and intelligence should combine to form a personality perfect in all respects, a harmonic whole, the natural contrast to and complement of man.

The culture of the courts became the model for that of the patricians in the towns. Since the late 15th century the families of the Florentine merchants and bankers, who had gained great wealth and political power, more and more modelled their ways on those of the nobility. Yet for the women the chances of any development were considerably more limited in these circles. Frequently they spent their childhood in the seclusion of a convent school, and in marriage they had to confine their activities to domestic duties. But the portrait busts by Desiderio da Settignano and Ghirlandajo's frescoes show the daughters of these houses as such self-assured and proud young ladies that one feels inclined to attribute to them wider interests than merely those of housewives. From the letters of Alessandra Macinghi degli Strozzi, a Florentine patrician, one gathers, however, that when choosing brides for her sons, she had other qualities in mind than culture and intellectual talents. Of importance to her were—besides the descent from a good family and a correspondingly large dowry—the reputation of the young girl, her virtue and pleasant manners; the young man's mother then personally examined the prospective bride to see whether she had a good figure, was well built with good flesh and skin, therefore not with a sickly pale face. It was further noted as an asset if she did not use any make-up and did not wear high-heeled shoes. It was mentioned of only one girl that she could read well; evidently this was not quite general. Alessandra Strozzi shows herself in her letters as an energetic and efficient housewife and business woman. She reported to her sons, when they were abroad, all economic and political events in the city, but intellectual problems or any topic concerning art were obviously quite alien to the sphere of her interests.

The culture of the patrician women seems to have been inferior to that of many a courtesan, as the more famous of these were able to vie with the great ladies at the courts in social manners and brilliant conversation.

The position of the women of the lower orders in Renaissance Italy was still the same as in the middle ages. In the late 15th century a Florentine bookseller describes it very clearly by taking the two main rules for the behaviour of women as derived from the teaching of St. Paul as a basis. He enumerates: "One: to bring up her children piously, and two: to be quiet in church, to which I myself would like to add: to be quiet everywhere else also."

The cultural ideal of the Humanists first influenced the neighbouring Latin countries. Among them was Portugal which, owing to its conquests overseas, had temporarily become the mightiest colonial power of Europe, with its trade expanding as far as Africa, Persia and India. Portuguese poets celebrated the beautiful women of Lisbon society. Princess Maria, daughter of Don Manuel I, had assembled around herself a circle of cultured women who spent their time in learned disputations. Aloysa Sigea from Toledo was said to be outstanding even among these ladies through her gift of rhetoric and her knowledge of languages. Emperor Maximilian was indebted for many important suggestions to his mother, a Portuguese princess, who was used to her homeland's wealth of spirited life.

In Spain learned women who were scholars in Greek and Latin, the Marchesa de Monteagudo doña Maria Pacheco de Mendoza, Isabella de Cordova are mentioned and, as master in rhetoric, Isabella de Rosere. Even in her mature age Queen Isabella took Latin lessons with Beatrix de Lagindo and read the classical authors. Yet the image of the Spanish women was still chiefly characterized by the ideals of the mediaeval knights' courtship. The ladies of the Iberian Peninsula knew how to fascinate men by beauty, grace and the mastery of dancing. Isabella, the Catholic, is said to have gone with her beautiful ladies-in-waiting to the battlefield, rousing the combatants by the mere sight of them to fight for victory.

In France the demand for an equal education for women had been formulated independently as early as the turn of the 14th century. Christina de Pisan, an Italian who lived in Paris at the court of the king, studied Plato and the Arabian sciences; in her fearless and radical writings she formulated Utopian demands for the emancipation of her sex which, however, were not to be realized at the time of the Renaissance. In the 16th century the Italian influence became decisive in all spheres. Francis I summoned artists and writers to France and thereby helped to inaugurate the Renaissance in his country. The development of humanism and Renaissance culture in France was due to a great extent to his sister Margaret, the wife of the King of Navarre. She was fluent in several languages, studied the philosophy of the ancients, wrote poetry and became the centre of the intellectual life of France, dedicated as it was to Neo-Platonism. Her court was, next to that of the king, the rallying point for all representatives of progressive ideas. Judging, however, from their correspondence, the majority of the ladies at court in Paris seemed more interested in the leading Italian fashions and the recipes for make-up than in the problems of the mind.

Lyon was the gate through which the Italian Renaissance entered France. There even women of the bourgeoisie—in particular Louise Labé, poetess and wife of a rope-maker—were thoroughly conversant with humanistic thought and asserted themselves in the circles of learned men.

The spread of humanism caused learning and education to be somewhat reformed also in the other countries north of the Alps. In the towns the middle class inhabitants aiming at universal culture formed the basis on which the Humanists, who lived among the burghers of the towns, built up their educational plans. For the women of the higher ranks they contemplated a humanistic education equal to that for men, in which the knowledge of the Greek and Latin languages and literatures was to follow upon elementary teaching. In England Sir Thomas Elyot advocated a higher education. But there again it was only the daughters of the first families who followed the example of their highly educated Queen Elizabeth and devoted themselves to the study of antiquity.

Basing his demand on Plato, Sir Thomas More in his *Utopia* called for complete equality of the sexes and for a higher education to be given to boys and girls in the same manner and to the same extent. With regard, however, to the learning of a trade, which was to be compulsory for all pupils, he allotted to the girls the specifically feminine occupations of the household—sewing, cooking and spinning. But with the exception of the model education of his own three daughters his ideas remained alien to the actual existing system of education for women. The same applies to the similar ideas of Erasmus of Rotterdam and to those of Juan Luis Vives, a Spanish doctor and Humanist who worked in the Netherlands. "Distaff and spindle are the woman's tools, and the Latin language is not suitable for womenfolk," is the answer given by the conservative abbot, in a dialogue written by Erasmus, to the woman who points to the noble ladies in Spain and Italy able to converse and dispute with any learned man. (34)

True, reading and writing seem to have been fairly common in towns, and quite a number of portraits painted by English or Netherlandish artists in the 16th century represent women or young girls with a book in their hands or writing a letter.

The education of the people was highly developed especially among the wealthy Netherlanders with their bourgeois policy, and often even the peasants were no longer illiterate. The women were commended by their contemporaries for their beauty and chastity and because they were keen on reading and writing, liked to quote from the Holy Scriptures, and could argue about dogma as well as the learned scholars (Guicciardini). This certainly furthered the spread of the Reformation.

The portrait of a young girl—probably belonging to the French nobility—holding in her hand an armillary sphere proves that like their Italian sisters some educated ladies of the north showed curiosity for contemporary technical and physical achievements, inventions and tools. In all likelihood this applied chiefly to the trading centres of all countries, which were in contact with all the world; universities were founded and science began to flourish there.

Yet as late as at the turn of the 16th century Aegidius Albertinus, 1560 – 1620, a Netherlandish writer and author of popular works stated in his *Weiblicher Lustgarten* (almanac for women), "As to what concerns the opinion that young girls or maidens ought to be encouraged to practise reading and writing, I found that there are divergent views. I for my part think it advisable for maidens to learn to read, to read good and pious books and to use them for their prayer. But as to writing, this is not at all to be recommended for women, especially as it enables them to write and to answer love letters ... Although some women might make good and creditable use of the art of writing, yet it is so much abused that it would be better to abolish it on the quiet..." (34)

In Germany highly educated women were to be met, as during the middle ages, chiefly in the convents. At that time these institutions had had the exclusive right to education and even at the turn of the 15th century this tradition still made itself felt, notwithstanding the moral decay spreading in many of the monasteries and convents. In some of the convents in south German towns several learned women even turned to the new humanistic studies, though limits were set to their interest in these "heathen sciences" by dogmatic rules.

Both sisters of the Humanist Willibald Pirckheimer, who lived as abbesses in the Convent of St. Clare at Nuremberg, were engaged in the study of the humanities and corresponded with many distant scholars. Their brother emphasized his affection for Caritas, because "she was more concerned with learning than with the customary life, and longed in particular for the occupation of the study of the humanities." He therefore dedicated to her his translation of Plutarch and she enjoyed reading this heathen work. She herself insisted that she was no scholar, only the friend of scholars. Nevertheless she admonished her teacher Celtis "to stop reading the base legendary tales of Diana, Venus, Jupiter and other accursed persons, whose souls are now tormented by the flames of hell."

Christoph Scheurl went so far as to compare the abbess with the famous Venetian Cassandra Fedele. All these eulogies, however, confirm the fact that this cultivated woman with her intellectual leanings was an exception which, outside the convents, was to be found almost solely in the families of the Humanists. Margarete Welser, the wife of the Humanist Michael Hummelburger of Ravensburg, is supposed to have made copies and extracts of Latin authors so that Peutinger could praise her and say: "Nothing is more rare and wonderful than when a woman tries to vie, with her erudition and eloquence, first in undecided contest with the most learned men, and then secures the prize of victory, although she is not born to this but to handle wool, to busy herself every day with practical work, to spin, to wear fine clothes and soft underclothes and to pursue the art of weaving. Seldom is there any woman in Swabia who does any good writing, wields a book instead of wool, the pen instead of the distaff, the stylus instead of the needle and not often is there one who does not cover her skin with make-up but the papyrus with a sequence of lines." He was exceedingly happy when he succeeded in marrying a girl of eighteen, who was "bashful, modest, lovely, respectable and somewhat conversant with the humanities," so that he had acquired a "companion and a disciple" for his studies. The education of his daughter also started in her early years: at the age of fourteen she was able to greet Emperor Maximilian as a conqueror with a public speech in Latin. (34)

It was an exception well worth mentioning when the chair of Greek at Heidelberg was given to a woman. This was the Italian Humanist Fulvia Morata Olympia, who had followed her husband, the doctor Andreas Gundler, from Ferrara to Germany.

The majority of women, however, had no possibility of improving their minds by dealing with the sciences.

Although burgher women and noblewomen took no small part in the spreading of the Reformation it led, at least in Lutheran countries, to a considerable restriction of the field of activities open to women, relegating them to household and family. Martin Luther commended marriage as an institution conformable to nature and therefore fought the celibacy ruling of the Church and introduced the marriage of priests; yet he saw the moral worth of the female sex only in the role of the faithfully caring housewife and mother. "To bring up the children and to look after the house, these are the tasks to which she has been called, has been created by God." He allotted no place to learning in the life of women, but said: "There is no coat or dress that suits a woman or young girl less well than when she tries to be

Family Lesson in Religion

clever." While the progressive theories of the Humanists were hardly ever realized in practice, the opinions of the Reformer were more effective, as they agreed with the general level of education, and probably also with the views of vast numbers of the population. His exclamation: "Would to God that each town had also a girls' school!" brought about the establishment of many new schools, but the teaching there was very limited and frequently reduced to one hour a day, while several hours were reserved for the teaching of boys. Religious instruction always stood in the foreground and to this were added only reading, writing and needlework. An ordinance of the Church published in the town of Northeim referred for its attitude even to antiquity: "For it is as necessary to educate the girls as well as the boys, since one can learn from history that among the Romans there were sometimes women who won the prize when competing with men in rhetoric."

But when in the year of 1528 the first school for girls was established in Brunswick with two hours daily of lessons containing plenty of religious teaching, this was everywhere deemed sufficient to make the girls into "useful, skilful, friendly, obedient, God-fearing and not self-willed housewives." Pious women of mature age were to be the teachers; by the Reformation these educational activities were made available in particular to former nuns from the dissolved convents—unless they married. Girls were allowed only in a few exceptional instances to visit the "big" schools, where Latin was taught.

In some isolated cases women of the ruling houses took an interest in the education of girls and saw to the foundation of schools for them. But even in the circles of the nobility the education of girls was frequently confined to the teaching of manners, piety and also needlework.

Outstanding among the princesses at German courts was Anna, the wife of Augustus, Elector of Saxony. In 1566 she established in Dresden a school for midwives, where she herself gave practical instruction, having given birth to fifteen children in thirty-seven years of marriage. She wrote a little book on medicines (*Arzneibüchlein*) and in 1581 founded the court pharmacy in Dresden. Moreover she is said to have shared the learned hobbies of her husband and, while experimenting in his laboratory, to have invented the once famous "white stomachic water." One may therefore assume that she really used her skilfully worked writing desk which is still preserved. (Ill. 77a)

MATRIMONY, MOTHERHOOD AND DOMESTIC LIFE

Visitors in the Lying-In-Room

Matrimony and family formed the predetermined and natural course of life for which the young girl was prepared and educated right from her childhood. She was trained in her earliest years in the running of the household with its manifold duties: often she learned to use distaff and spindle at the age of five, and her mother soon made her join all other domestic activities. An early marriage was the rule and was eagerly desired, since for unmarried daughters nothing was left but to enter a convent.

The aristocratic and the patrician families used to arrange for their unmarried daughters to be admitted to one of the orders of high standing or, after the Reformation, to enter as a canoness one of the institutions for unmarried gentlewomen, where they were accommodated according to their rank. The daughters of peasants and day-labourers had to spend their lives as servants or to dedicate themselves to the care of the poor and the sick in the more unpretentious convent-like institutions such as that of the Beguines.

It was therefore usual for girls to get married at the age of fifteen or sixteen. In the course of the Reformation the marriageable age was sometimes fixed at eighteen years for women and twenty for men, as for example, by the Consistory of Meissen. As a matter of course husband and wife were chosen exclusively from among members of the social rank to which they themselves had belonged from birth. In the families of the nobility and the ruling houses this choice was based by the parents on political or dynastic considerations and the betrothal as a rule arranged while the partners were still children. At the age of thirteen or fourteen the bride was conducted to her future husband whom often she had not previously seen.

Among the burghers, economic circumstances, family and financial means were also decisive, not inclination or beauty. Usually the marriage was arranged between members of the same trade or guild; the journeyman proposed to the daughter of his master, hoping thereby to secure for himself the way to an independent existence. For the same reason the masters' widows, too, were much sought after even by young men. The guilds made matrimony compulsory for the masters, and certain duties forming part of her husband's trade devolved upon his wife, for instance the selling of the goods made by him, and the feeding of the apprentices and journeymen. Quite often, therefore, young men married old women

20

and vice versa for financial or professional reasons; many pictures of the times show such ill-assorted couples, clearly pointing to the underlying financial motives. (Ill. 27)

Seldom did a brave couple break down the barriers of rank, yet this did happen sometimes: a nobleman might marry the daughter of a rich member of the bourgeoisie, as the patricians in the towns were much respected at that time and were enabled by their wealth to lead a life consonant with that of the nobility. On the other hand marriage between the children of peasants and burghers were much less frequent and could happen only in smaller towns with a partly rural economy. One marriage of the 16th century which caused a great sensation was that in 1557 of the beautiful Philippine Welser, daughter of a patrician in Augsburg, and Archduke Ferdinand II of the Tirol, a love match greatly romanticized in legend and literature. Emperor Ferdinand I insisted that this union of his son should be kept secret, and the children of a permanently happy marriage had to renounce all claims to inheritance. Not before 1576 was the secrecy lifted and the marriage declared legal and valid by Pope Gregory XIII. Archduke Ferdinand assigned to his wife some of his property, for instance the castle of Ambras near Innsbruck; he also cared for his wife's family by providing a fair number of them with places of authority.

The barriers separating the ranks were, however, frequently removed for the benefit of the numerous illegitimate sons and daughters of princes and noblemen. An adequate education was provided for them and they were often given suitable titles. The usual and frequent love affairs of the men of these circles included noblewomen as well as burghers' daughters, also peasant women and maids; they were responsible for a large number of illegitimate children. By contrast love affairs between noblewomen and men of inferior rank were criticized much more rigorously. The love-couples shown in drawings and paintings are usually clothed in costumes indicating that they both belong to the same rank; only the love between equals could be guaranteed to lead eventually to a marriage sanctioned by the Church and accepted by society.

The decisive voice in choosing the matrimonial partner belonged to the parents. Even sons often let their mothers choose a suitable wife for them. The correspondence between Alessandra Strozzi and her children while they were away from home is eloquent proof of the energy with which this widow of a Florentine patrician tried—over the years, with the help of friends—to arrange good marriages not only for her daughters but also for her sons. Church attendance then offered her opportunities to observe carefully for herself the candidates who had seemed suitable by their origin, dowry and personal respectability, and to find out whether they would also prove satisfactory in appearance. In addition to this, she made use of the services of professional matrimonial agents to find the right partners for her children.

By agreement between the two families a mutual promise of marriage—the betrothal—was brought about; usually it was preceded by the signing of a regular matrimonial contract, which stipulated the size of the bride's dowry. As Alessandra Strozzi observed when one of her daughters was married: "The man who takes a wife expects cash." (68)

In 1424 an insurance institute was founded in Florence which guaranteed a dowry in cash to the legitimate children of Florentine citizens; it gradually developed into a kind of savings-bank for dowries. When a daughter was born, the father gave through this institution a certain sum to the state which was paid out, with interest and compound interest, when the girl was married. The interest was so high that a fivefold amount was returned after fifteen years, that is at the marriageable age usual for girls in Florence. This sum was given to the husband. If the girl had died or remained unmarried, half of the money went to the state, which in this way tried to compound its increasing debts; nor did marriages at a later age bring about any increase of the amount paid out. This institution was equally popular with patricians and with artisans, and most families made use of it. It therefore aroused great indignation when Lorenzo de Medici, because of his growing financial difficulties, made some changes concerning those *monti delle dotti;* after 1485 only part of the amount due was paid out to the husband in cash, the rest was credited with an interest of seven percent. (68)

Moreover, each girl had to contribute a dowry adequate to her rank, which consisted of the household linen and also of the requirements for the care of the expected children. As a rule the parents supplied the "bride's chest" to hold the dowry; decorated with elaborate carvings, inlay or paintings, it formed the most important piece of Renaissance furniture.

Some boards from these chests, called *cassone* in Italy, are still to be found in many museums as they were often painted by first rate artists with love-scenes from antiquity.

The marriage portions, too, which the bridegroom had to contribute, were sometimes fixed by contract: he had at least to equip the bride with sumptuous garments. When all points of business were settled, the promise of marriage took place before witnesses. This was the formal betrothal recognized as binding by the Church and the civic authorities; usually some kind of ceremony was connected with it. The bridegroom put a ring on the hand of his bride, often on the day of the betrothal but, if not, on the wedding day. The plain modern wedding-ring was not known at the time of the Renaissance, valuable golden rings with precious stones were used. Usually there were inscriptions in the ring, the most popular was: "What God hath joined, let no man put asunder." Wedding regulations fixed maximum prices for the wedding-rings which the two partners gave to each other. The ring was worn on the fourth finger of the right hand, as it was assumed that this finger was connected directly with the heart by a special vein, the *vena amoris*.

The exchange of presents between bridegroom and bride was customary for the period of the engagement. In Germany the bride often gave her young husband the "wedding shirt" made by herself. The so-called "bath shirt" was a relic of earlier times, when a ceremonial bath was taken by the bridal couple immediately before the wedding. A decree of Nuremberg of 1557 mentions also the gift of white linen to be presented by the bride to the groom: so-called "shaving cloths," for the house-barber and *Fazinetlein* (handkerchiefs). The bride was given chiefly jewelry or clothes. The amount these betrothal presents reached in the wealthy circles of the patricians can be gauged from the diary of the Florentine silk merchant Marco Parente. With a merchant's precision he noted under the date of 12th January 1458: fourteen sumptuous garments and all the other things, which he had given to his bride and which he had had valued for 165 florins. The lovely sixteen-year-old Caterina Strozzi received according to this: "A long upper garment with hanging sleeves of white damask, bordered with marten; an upper garment with hanging sleeves of the whitest thin silk, embroidered and bordered with marten; an upper garment of white wool

with tight sleeves of green velvet; a dress, dark blue, with sleeves of green velvet; a dark blue dress with sleeves of velvet from Alessandria; sixteen ells of red cloth from Lucca; seventeen shirts completely finished; ten towels in one piece; thirty handkerchiefs; thirty childrens' handkerchiefs; one ell of white damask; two large towels; a basin and a chest with a compass and the crest of the Strozzi and my own; a prayer book; a chain of large corals; two small knives with sheaths of silver to be worn at the belt; a grey belt with silver decorations; six silk berets; three needle boxes." (68)

There follows a list of the presents of which the value is not specifically stated and a bouquet of peacock feathers as a present for the wedding day, decorated with silver and pearls. More costly presents are then enumerated separately, each with its price. The mother could therefore say proudly that her daughter would carry, when leaving the house, more than four hundred florins on her person. She admitted, however, at the same time that she had had to take the thousand florins for the dowry partly from her own, partly from her son's capital, as otherwise the wedding could not have taken place in the year for which it had been planned. She also mentioned that to have married her daughter into a still better family would have cost four to five hundred florins more, and that such a step upwards does not necessarily bring happiness to a girl but often only worry.

The marriage portion of a bridegroom from the artisan class was of course more modest; yet the list of the fabrics, shawls, hair-ribbons and pieces of jewelry which the Florentine Landucci gave to his young wife is long enough; but it consists mainly of simple materials and trimmings, which had still to be made up into garments.

The luxury shown at their marriage by the ladies of the nobility even surpassed that of the patricians. There was a large number of dresses and often each one cost a fortune. The Polish philosopher Nicolaus Rej therefore gave warning of the claims which a lady of fashion of his country would make on the house of her future husband: "For the coach he will need red cloth and bear skins right up to the knees, carpets must hang out of the coach on both sides and decorative bells shaped like apples shine everywhere. He has to have two lady's maids and a third one who watches over them like a hen over her chickens, and on the dress of each of them there must be a threefold trimming. He must put hangings on the walls and no *sauerkraut* is to appear on his table. When a guest arrives, he has to be welcomed with great ceremonies; wine is indispensable and a picture of Christ's Crucifixion has to be painted on his glass; rice pudding has to form part of the evening meal, as pot barley no longer suits the mistress of the house. To say nothing of a visit by the father-in-law: when he arrives with some fifty horses, six dishes must at once be served and drinks to be poured out to all alike, as each of them will wear a collar of fox fur and it will be difficult to know who is a gentleman." (30)

The marriage was solemnized in a church and was taken for indissoluble by Catholics and Protestants. Like most other notable events in life the wedding was always celebrated with elaborate festivities. Feasting started on the prior evening or on the morning of the wedding day; the main festivity began after the church ceremony and often went on for several days. It took place in the house either of the bride's parents or of the bridegroom's, sometimes in an inn or in the town hall. Even people of lesser means invited fifty or more guests. In many regions the guests were invited by a professional "inviter" and numbered several hundreds in well-to-do families. The entertainments included music and dancing and sometimes pageants, masquerades and manifold games. Weddings of the nobility were turned into small public festivities, in which the neighbouring villages took part, and princely marriages were followed by rowdy festivals, usually lasting for a whole week.

The costs of festivities of this kind were excessively high, and several towns limited, by decrees, the expenses for weddings according to the rank of the families. Sumptuous dresses added to the cost of entertaining, as everybody wanted to show off with them especially on such a day. Sometimes the bridegroom had to pay not only for the expensive attire of the bride, but also for the dresses of the bridesmaids. The guests, too, had special robes made for the festivities and brought presents—objects of fancywork like dishes or small chests painted for the particular occasion have been preserved until today. The goldsmiths of Nuremberg invented the so-called bride's goblets, representing a woman who holds a cup in her hand and whose wide skirt forms another beaker; to drink from one of these vessels, without spilling from the other, was one of the most popular party games to test the skill of the guests, played while sitting at the table. Another pastime during the many courses of the meal consisted in the recitation of wedding poems, the singing of piquant songs and the proposing of toasts.

When the bride had been led by relatives and friends to the house of her husband in a solemn procession, often to the accompaniment of music, everyday married life began for her. Its most intimate problems, like all questions of sex, were discussed quite freely, even in writing. A large family was most welcome, so that there usually were a great number of births. Childless women with substantial means took the baths at some resort or prayed in pilgrimages for help against sterility. Notwithstanding the high rate of mortality of infants and young children, six, eight, ten, sometimes even fifteen and more children grew up in many families. Motherhood and confinement therefore played a prominent role in a woman's life. This happy event recurred nearly every year; welcome as it was, it yet was permanently fraught with great danger since, owing to the prevailing conditions of hygiene and the scanty knowledge of medicine, complications or fever frequently spelt death for the mother. When all turned out well, the mother used to stay at home for six weeks, that is, until her first churchgoing. Visits to the woman in confinement were one of the foremost social duties for women.

Numerous pictorial representations of biblical themes provide information about the customs usually observed in the lying-in room, as the artists did not reproduce the stories in a manner faithful to history but tried to enliven them and to enhance the effect by transferring them to their own time. A great many pictures of the birth of Mary, or of St. John, dating from the 15th and 16th centuries therefore constitute an inexhaustible source of knowledge showing us the arrival of the new-born child in a typical bourgeois environment with all the details of the lying-in room and the women occupied there. Furthermore, there are detailed descriptions in the books for the use of midwives, often illustrated with woodcuts by eminent artists like Jost Amman and Hans Burgkmair. These books describe precisely the birth itself, for which it was customary to use the delivery-chair. A midwife was always present and several experienced neighbours were there to assist her if necessary. Physicians were not consulted, not even for difficult cases; recourse was taken rather to the barber. Only in the families of princes of the very first rank was a physician in ordinary sometimes allowed to take charge. The duty

23

of private baptism of weak children also devolved upon the midwife. Men had no access to the lying-in room. In Valais, Switzerland, however, "the men were compelled to stand by their wives while in labour, so that they must later be more patient with them." (74)

Already in the 16th century great care was taken of the training of midwives. The physician Eucharius Rösslin dedicated his book, *Der Swangeren Frauwen und Hebammen Rosengarten* (Almanac for Pregnant Women and Midwives), Strasbourg, 1513, to the Duchess Catherine of Brunswick and Lüneburg, requesting her to distribute it among respectable and pious women and midwives in Germany. Anna, the wife of the Elector of Saxony, specially asked Martin Pfinzing in Nuremberg to recommend to her "a pious, devout, modest and experienced midwife," who had a well-grounded knowledge and could teach the women in Saxony. She founded a school for midwives as she realized that "many pregnant women, women in confinement and small children of noble as well as of common rank are often miserably neglected, injured, harmed and crippled at the time of the birth or in the following six weeks, all through the clumsiness, arrogance and rashness of the midwives and assisting women; few sensible midwives are to be found in this country." (7) The Duchess Dorothea Sybilla of Brieg composed together with her "old Grete," an experienced midwife, a treatise: *Gemeiner Rath an Schwangere und Gebärende, auch in sunst allerlei Krankheit, sunderlich auf den Dörfern heilsamb zu gebrauchen* (General Advice to Pregnant Women and Women in Childbed and also in Various Other Illnesses, especially Useful for Villages). She herself bore the cost of the printing and distribution of the booklet. (7) According to her instructions all kinds of old superstitious customs were still to be used during labour; to facilitate it, henbane had to be tied to the left hip; ground laurel leaves to be laid upon the navel, hydromel or pounded myrrh to be taken in wine. (7)

In the contemporary pictorial representations the mother is seen lying on a broad bed with a canopy in a burgher's living-room. A midwife or a servant offers her an invigorating dish while women, often assembled in large numbers, bathe the child, swaddle it and lay it in the cradle already provided. Sometimes the first milk of the mother, a fresh egg as a symbol of fertility, or a silver coin were added to the child's first bath. Frequently astrologers were asked to come to the house to cast the

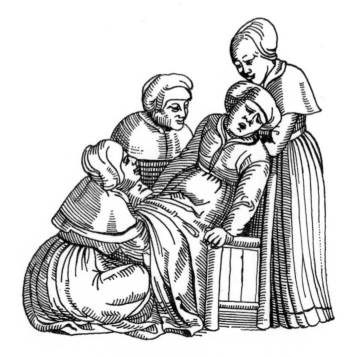

horoscope for the new-born child. The women from the neighbourhood and the vicinity came in great numbers to visit the woman while she was lying-in and to bring her presents. In Italy there were special salvers on which the presents were offered, called *desci da parto*. Originally they were used to carry the food or the fruit to be offered, but gradually these plates themselves were decorated with valuable paintings and used as gifts. A round salver of this kind, painted by Masaccio, shows a scene in a lying-in room in a stately patrician house where a salver just like the one shown in the painting is carried in solemn procession to the woman in childbed. (Ill. 31 b) Majolica dishes, too, were specially made as childbed presents, usually showing scenes of confinement. The visitors were offered a cup of welcome; judging by some drawings this was sometimes extended in Germany to a small feast; in an engraving by Dürer, representing the birth of Mary, a large jug is seen passing from hand to hand.

At the princely courts the new-born child was as a rule fed and cared for by a wet-nurse, as shown in a painting by François Clouet. (Ill. 45) In patrician Florence, too, it was usual to take a wet-nurse into the house or even to send the infant into the country to some peasant woman, to make sure it would thrive. Among the lower orders the mother herself nursed her child. This too is shown by images of the Virgin; studies from nature are seldom to be found with the exception, for instance, of sketches by a north Italian artist of the early 15th century, whose work has fortunately been preserved. (Ill. 44)

The care and education of the children as they grew up from infancy was the task of the women; the teaching of religion and of manners and, as far as girls were concerned, that of domestic work and sewing also formed part of the mother's duties. Ante-nuptial children also often lived in the family. In the ranks of the artisans they had, however, to suffer all through their life from the blemish of illegitimate birth and were usually not allowed to learn any trade organised by a guild, while in contrast with this the patricians and the nobility conceded to them activities and matrimony in accordance with their parents' rank.

For all women the duties in kitchen and house were at that time very extensive, whether a woman was working herself or supervising the work of one or more maids. One of her regular duties besides cooking and baking was, for instance, the dipping of candles. Even ladies of noble or princely rank took charge of the preparation of food themselves. Philippine Welser was known as a master-cook and her recipes, filling one hundred and thirty-six pages, represent one of the oldest and best cookery-books (73). Netherlandish artists of the 16th century have recorded in their pictures of kitchens this very important part of the women's work. Biblical subjects, for example the wedding of Cana, or Christ visiting Martha and Mary, show kitchens in great detail, even with their less important chores. But Pieter Aartsen the painter and his disciple Joachim Beuckelaer were the first to display cooks and maids at work and to put these simple women into the foreground as large single figures. (Ill. 57)

One of the important activities of the female members of the family of all ranks was the spinning of wool and flax. In the country the spinning rooms formed the meeting-point for the women on the long winter evenings and quite frequently men joined in the entertainments. The wives of the artisans in the towns also sat at the distaff. The pursuit of this specially feminine handicraft was looked upon as an honourable occupation for the women of the higher classes, too; they even liked to be portrayed while thus engaged. The ladies at the court of Ferrara can therefore be seen at the spindle, the embroidery frame or the loom. (Ill. 42) The weaving of cloth had been given for some considerable time to weavers who were members of the guild; the very fine fabrics were imported into Italy from abroad, but the linen for the household and for the dowry of the daughters was produced in the wealthy families of the Florentine patriciate by the mistress of the house. Alessandra Strozzi ordered particularly good and yet inexpensive flax from abroad, spun it and then gave it to the weaver; the bleaching of the linen and the sewing of the shirts and the towels for her sons she then undertook herself.

In many houses the housewife was to be met at the loom, as Pinturicchio depicted her in his fresco of the Return of Ulysses. Most women also made their own clothes; only those worn on festive occasions were sometimes made in the tailor's workshop: because of their costliness and the durability of the material they had often to last for the woman's whole life. (Ill. 34a)

In many houses the entertainments in the family circle during the leisure hours, in the evenings and on holidays included music; there was community singing or the daughters alone joined in a duet or trio, and it

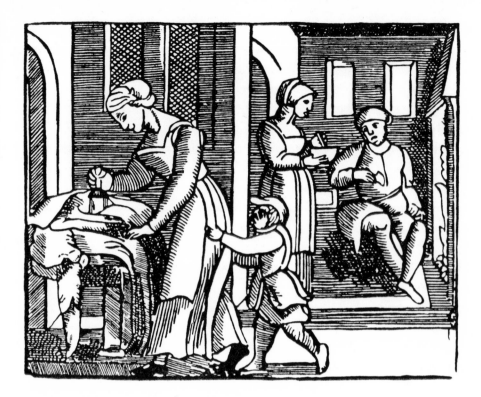

was not uncommon for them to play an instrument, the lute or the clavichord. Women were the partners of the men also in the dice, card or board games, which were often played passionately, and women and young girls took part in the ball games and in other out-of-door entertainments, favoured chiefly in court circles.

Riding and hunting formed one of the favourite activities of the noblewomen in all countries. Beatrice d'Este, the sports-loving sister of Isabella, surpassed her husband in the pursuit of falconry; she owned a valuable collection of hunting equipment and implements. The ladies participating in the hunts might also have enjoyed the feasts connected with them; in the 16th century the women shared in the men's drinking bouts, nor did they take exception to coarse jokes. The drinking of wine and beer had spread particularly in Germany to the women of all circles. The Duke of Gotha felt even compelled to issue a "drinking order for the princely woman."

Change was provided in the life of the townspeople by the fairs and carnivals with their booths, conjurors and musicians, among whom there used also to be some women. In the villages the country fairs supplied similar amusements. Only a few women were able to leave the domain of their homes. Because of the bad and unsafe roads and the inadequate inns, travelling was very tiring and therefore reserved for the men, who had to under-

take it for the sake of their professions as merchants, wandering journeymen or artists. It was an exception when Dürer took his wife Agnes with him on his journey to the Netherlands. Only noblewomen travelled with their own coaches to neighbouring courts to take part there in family festivities, the reception of foreign guests or other similar events.

Already at the time of the Renaissance women of the wealthy bourgeoisie were sometimes able to benefit by travels to health resorts. Especially were visited places with curative waters, which served to prevent or to cure illnesses, though they also provided a pleasant social life and offered entertainments in the baths themselves which were enjoyed in company. Remedial cures in these resorts were prescribed to women against sterility, and the Tirolese hot springs were supposed to cure various female diseases. For the women of the lower ranks pilgrimages were the only enterprises of this kind they could afford, provided they were not afraid of the hardships of tramping and insecure lodgings.

In domestic everyday life there was, of course, no lack of matrimonial quarrels, with which we are familiarized through satirical representations in many a graphic work. The women's complaints of their husbands and the husbands' complaints of their wives were caricatured in pamphlets which were widely distributed with explanatory texts. The subjugated husband and the enslaved lover, in particular, were described in many variants. The ancient story of Aristotle who let himself be used as a riding horse by his idolized Phyllis was very popular. There was, however, also the story of Pyramus and Thisbe as an instance of faithful love; it was painted by Albrecht Altdorfer as the contemporary romance of a German mercenary soldier and a young burgher-girl.

Everywhere adultery was counted among the punishable crimes, as both Church and state thought themselves called upon to safeguard the matrimonial bond, contracted only in church. As a rule women who succumbed to temptation were punished more severely than men, although often the latter, too, did not escape penalties; such "cavalier delicts" were overlooked only with regard to noblemen. In Hesse the *Reformationssatzung*, a decree issued in 1572 jointly by the Church and the police, provided the death penalty for both partners in case of a twofold adultery; the heavy penalties of the time also sent many a thief to the gallows. In practice, the magistrates only put the adulterers in the pillory or banished them temporarily from the town, but a few examples mention the drowning of women who had been guilty of this crime. Yet notwithstanding the threat of harsh punishment, adultery does not seem to have been un-

common and was frequent especially in Italian society: the contemporary novels are full of love-affairs, in which both married men and women indulged and at which people smiled in good-tempered derision. On the other hand the austere life of Elisabetta Gonzaga was held up for admiration, or that of Isabella d'Este, who remained faithful to her husband although he was continually embroiled in love-affairs.

Divorce was unknown at that time. Sir Thomas More advocated in his *Utopia* divorce and re-marriage, but these theories failed to gain ground in practice. Only in the highest circles, in princely and royal houses, was it sometimes possible to gain the Church's permission for a divorce, which made it allowable to contract another marriage, usually in the interest of the dynasty. The best-known example of this is the divorce of two of the six marriages of Henry VIII of England. It was moreover customary for a great gentleman to entertain a permanent mistress side by side with his wife. The Reformers, notwithstanding their otherwise severe morality, allowed bigamy in certain situations rather than a divorce. For instance, they gave permission to Landgrave Philip of Hesse, 1504—1567, to be married legally to two women, his already lawful wife and a young lady-in-waiting. But as a rule a second marriage could be contracted only after the death of one of the partners of the first.

PHYSICAL CULTURE AND COSMETICS — FASHION AND JEWELRY

Beauty culture filled a large part of the women's life in the Renaissance. Italy set the fashion for the whole of Europe. A well-tended outward appearance formed part of the image of the *Gentildonna*. Woman's beauty was glorified by the poets, ideals were set up and fixed in every detail, and women were anxious to approximate as closely as possible to these literary ideals. The ladies of the upper classes of society were expected to show not learning, good social manners and charm alone, but also taste and the ability to enhance their appearance with clothes, coiffure and cosmetics. All means were permissible to retain the ideal picture of youthfully smooth beauty and to represent the requisite type with fair hair and clear skin. No trouble seemed too great to obtain, through protracted bleaching, the desired golden colour of the hair—mostly dark by nature—and to feign a white complexion with the help of make-up and powder. Recipes for cosmetics and perfumes, partly invented by the ladies themselves, were jealously kept secret, though sometimes they were exchanged in letters.

Some women experimented on themselves with ever new ointments and perfumes. Isabella d'Este, famous for so many other qualities was also a past master in the invention of perfumes. Fragrant creams, her own "compositions," which she dispatched in small but precious containers of boxwood, horn, crystal, gold or silver, were famous and greatly in demand as far away as in France. Caterina Sforza, known for her manly courage, has left a written code of her *Experimenti*, of which a copy dated 1525 has been preserved. It describes a very large number of perfumes, cosmetics and medicines, giving exact prescriptions, most of them her own invention: several of them are for beautifying waters, various mixtures to make the skin white, some to make the hair grow, and others to remove unwanted hair, hints for the bleaching and dyeing of hair, suggestions as to how to curl it, how to make the teeth white and how to keep the gums firm and rosy.

In all other countries, too, the women, in particular those of the nobility, were anxious to improve their appearance. In his satirical book, *De incertitudine et vanitate scientiarum et artium*, published 1532 in Cologne, Cornelius Agrippa of Nettesheim compared the woman at court with the Egyptian temples which, beautifully painted and decorated on the outside, contained nothing but a monkey, a goat or a cat. He asserted moreover that their conversation revolved exclusively on questions of

Bathing Couple in Tub

fashion, how to dye and to put up the hair, which were the best folds for the garments... (30)

Regarding the basis of all physical culture, the use of water and soap, less is handed down in the literature or the pictures from the Latin countries than about the bathing practices in the north. One might, however, assume cleanliness to have been rather greater in Italian society, as there certain scented soaps formed much coveted toilet requisites, greatly welcomed as requested gifts when brought back from afar. The Italians were therefore very critical of other countries. They mentioned the lack of cleanliness in France and the bad smell even in the royal apartments. Guido Postumo, an Italian visiting France, reported to Isabella d'Este in a letter of 1511: "The women here are rather dirty, frequently with some itch on the hands and several other kinds of filth; but to make up for this, they have pretty faces, lovely flesh and are charming when they speak; besides they are very willing to be kissed, touched and embraced" (39). On the other hand there is, evidently contradicting this, the picture of Diane de Poitiers in her bath, surrounded by her nurse and servants; it shows the bath in a tub as a luxurious pleasure, enjoyed by the great lady in company. The mistress of Henry II of France was famous, even in her old age, for her lovely complexion, which was explained by her particular bathing practices, her daily cold washings and baths in milk. There are other French paintings and tapestries, from approximately 1500, showing bathing women to whom sweets are offered or who are entertained with music; yet this was certainly limited to court circles.

A more intimate bathing scene is that of Hans Memling's picture of Bathsheba; it takes us to the Netherlands where the bourgeoisie was gaining importance. Here the bathtub is completely enclosed in a kind of tent and only one servant stands by, ready to assist her mistress when she steps out of the bath. (Ill. 61)

Paintings and drawings afford a still clearer insight into the pleasures of public bathing. In the middle ages public bathrooms were a popular institution in all European countries. They were frequently visited but at the same time notorious as men and women bathed there together in large tubs, while food and drinks were served to them. Under the supervision of the barber, sweating-baths and vapour-baths were available, and one could be washed and massaged by "bathservants" and "bathgirls."

As the entertainments in these bath establishments, often lasting for hours, were hardly to be distinguished from those in the brothels, they fell into disrepute at the time of the Reformation. Owing to the influence exercised by the Protestant clergy, the public baths were closed down in several towns, especially as with epidemics spreading fast they formed a dangerous source of infection. This, however, probably led to a deterioration of the general cleanliness, as there were private bathrooms only in the houses of the patricians or in the palaces of the nobility, while elsewhere a tub had to suffice. In view of the bad hygienic conditions and the immense quantity of dirt in the streets alone, it is not surprising that Hieronymus Gardanus, who died in 1576, complained in his Memoirs: "Men and women, even those who are thought to be pleasing, teem with fleas and lice, stink from their arm-pits, others from their feet, most of them from their mouths." It is significant that because of the extent of this plague of vermin, fur collars were called, even in Italy, "little flea furs."

On the other hand, drawings from the early 16th century describe some public baths with separate accommodation for the sexes, which women could use for a thorough care of their bodies and the washing of their hair. They took their children to these baths and while they washed them the mothers asked to be cupped by the barber.

Medicinal baths were already known in the 16th century and journeys to healing springs were quite frequent.

At Leuk in Switzerland, famous for its mineral water, men and women bathed together in a large basin in the open air and enjoyed at the same time wine and food. The ladies like the men wore no clothes, but sometimes their jewelry or fashionable berets. In the early 15th century the Florentine G. F. Poggio described the high spirits of the people taking the baths at Baden in the Swiss canton of Aargau: "All who want to make love, all who want to marry or who otherwise look out for pleasure, they all come here where they find what they are looking for."

A little Swiss song starts significantly with the following verse:

Es will e Frau uf Bade go
und will de Ma nit noche lo.
(A woman wants to go to Baden,
But does not want her husband to follow her.)

Another song of the 16th century about the journeys to bathing resorts, called *Badenfahrt*, runs:

Ich bin gen Baden zogen
Zu lösen ab meine Brunst,
So find ich mich betrogen,
Denn es ist gar umsunst...
(I have gone to Baden
To get rid of my heats.
I find myself cheated,
For it was quite in vain) (46)

A painting by Lucas Cranach depicts the contemporary notion of the fountain of youth, where old women hoped to be rejuvenated. Swimming, the rejuvenated women leave the large basin and at once turn to the enjoyments of life.

The care of the teeth, and of the fingernails and toenails was customary at least in the higher ranks of society. Tooth-powder seems to have been generally known; in a letter by Emilia Pia to Isabella d'Este we read of a mouth-wash "of the kind which was used by the Queens of Naples; it ought to be applied in the following manner; when the teeth are clean, one keeps a little of it in the mouth, just as much as seems right, but it must not be cold. As I send you only very little of it, Your Excellency could dip a small wad in it, and with that moisten your teeth and gums as often as you like..." (39) Manicure consisted in the cutting and polishing of the nails. Isabella d'Este ordered for it from Venice "a small pair of damascened scissors, sharp and pointed, as we want to use them to cut the fingernails." In 1505 her friend Emilia Pia sent her a piece of wood, "which has the property of giving the fingernails a very high shine when used in the following way: one rubs its leather-covered side for so long on the nails until one feels some warmth, and then it gives the bright shine..." (39) Several ladies of Italian society wore gloves at night, so as to keep their skin soft and white.

Great pains were taken by the women of the Renaissance in the care and treatment of the hair. It was washed with perfumed essences, and often the whole day was dedicated to this and the subsequent drying. The dyeing of the hair was quite general, used in various ways sometimes even by men. As fair hair was preferred everywhere and praised by the poets, the women from the South especially with their naturally dark hair were

keen to brighten it up artificially. There were the most varied recipes and methods for this. Caterina Sforza describes in her *Experimenti* a distillate made from the ashes of peeled beech-wood, in which the hair had to be washed repeatedly and then dried in the sun. For the complicated and lengthy bleaching, the women of Venice used their galleries, square structures of wood shaped like arcades, which stood on the roofs of the houses. Vecellio, a contemporary, gives a vivid description in his book on costumes: "To make their hair look fair, the Venetian women spend as much time on their galleries as in their bedrooms, and expose their head the whole day to the sun. Usually they sit there when the sun is hottest, and moisten their head with a small sponge fastened to the point of a spindle. They dip it in a water they either buy or make themselves. This they repeat every time the sun has dried their hair. They make it thereby as fair as it is whenever we see them. They wear, for this procedure, straw hats which have no crown and are called *solana;* their brim is so broad that it protects the faces from the sun, while the hair can be spread out upon it." (25)

The custom of bleaching the hair was not restricted to Italy; the ladies in northern countries, too, tried to give a lighter shade to their hair and to put it into the chosen coiffure although this usually meant squeezing it under a bonnet. Sebastian Brant in *The Ship of Fools*, published in 1494, scoffs at them: "They grease themselves with monkey fat, they puff out their hair with sulphur and resin and by breaking the white of an egg into it, they make it so stiff that it can be given any desired shape; they put their heads out of the window so as to bleach the hair in the sun."

According to the ideal of the Italian Renaissance fair hair should be matched by dark eyes and dark eyebrows, which were plucked to form beautifully curved arcs. In the 15th century they were completely plucked out, and this was done also to the foremost hair, pushing back the hair-line to make the forehead appear higher.

As there was not always enough of the woman's own hair to form the elaborate coiffures fashionable in Italy since the late 15th century, and worn mostly without bonnets, false hair came into use. Coiffures made up or partly made up of it are easily distinguished in some of the portraits. Casola, a Milanese priest, reported in his diary of 1494 about the hairdresses of the women in Venice: "The most part of these consists of false hair; I know this for certain, as I have seen masses of it hung up on clothes' lines in the Piazza di San Marco, where the peasants sell it." (25) Wigs of real hair or of white or yellow silk formed a part of the luxury articles which were burned at the stake when preachers like Savonarola in Florence had preached repentance, and moved their consciences, thus inducing the ladies to shun earthly pomp—although, in the majority of cases, for a short time only.

German contemporary sources report complaints that natural hair was no good, as it had to be bleached, and that the women therefore preferred to wear "fine, large, thick, yellow borrowed or purchased plaits." In pictures, however, most of the hair is hidden under bonnets or berets, which makes it all the more surprising that great efforts were taken to form an elaborate coiffure.

Abundant quantities of make-up were used to achieve the appearance of youthful beauty unspoiled by wrinkles. There were mixtures for all parts of the body, even for eyelids and teeth, so that poets and writers often turned with quite drastic expressions against the excessive use of these beautifiers, as their content of sublimate, especially mercury, threatened to harm the skin and to blacken the teeth. A report by a man from Ferrara has been handed down to us; his sister lost all her skin through the application of an ointment.

Usually the ladies painted their face, their neck and the upper part of their chest to give the complexion the desired light shades. In Italy even the country girls tried hard for it and asked for cosmetics and white lead to be brought out to them from town.

It was also the general practice in other parts of Europe to paint the face with white lead and ointments containing mercury to acquire a refined pale complexion. Cosmetics of this kind were used even by the patrician ladies of Cologne notwithstanding their black high-necked dresses and their large starched bonnets, which made them look almost like nuns: before his identity was established their portraitist Barthel Bruyn the Younger was called the "Master of the Pale Faces." Juan Luis Vives, the Spanish Humanist, philosopher and pedagogue in Louvain and Bruges felt induced to proceed energetically in his *Instruction for a Christian Woman*, 1544, against this abuse and to call it unworthy of a Christian woman.

Manifold recipes for make-up and ointments have been preserved in Italy, simple ones for more general use and some extremely expensive ones, the making of which was often accompanied by superstitious customs. Alessandro Piccolomini describes the preparation of a cosmetic in his *Dialogue*, published in 1539: "One takes solid silver and mercury pressed through chamois leather and mixes them and, after adding some fine sugar, grinds them a whole day long, always in the same direction; this mixture is then taken out of the mortar and ground by a painter on a porphyry slab, mixing kneaded silver and pearls into it, whereupon it has again to be grated on porphyry. It is then returned to the mortar and one dilutes it in the morning before breaking one's fast; chewed mastic and a little sweet almond oil have to be added. In this liquid condition it has to be stirred for a day, then to be mixed with ashroot water, to be poured into a bottle and brought to the boil in a hot water bath. This has to be done four times, each time with fresh water. The fifth time the water is kept separate and the mixture put in a bowl of stone where one lets it set. The liquid of the mixture is then carefully skimmed off, and at the bottom remains the sublimate to which milk is added, which eventually is scented with musk and ambergris." (25)

In addition to the paints and ointments there were perfumed waters, oils, pomades, and most important of all, perfumes, which were sold by all druggists. The craze for fragrant scents came from the Orient, spread quickly, and led in the 16th century to the heyday of perfumery in Italy, especially in Florence. The druggists in all European countries ordered from there what they could not produce themselves. As the demand for perfumes to overcome the smell of uncleanliness increased steadily, druggists more and more often themselves extracted fragrant scents from flowers, fruits, roots or leaves, and mixed them with liquid wax, pig's fat or oil. Rose-water and orange-water, musk, nutmeg, ambergris, lavender, moschatel, benzoin and many other strong scents were equally popular. People sprinkled themselves with them, sometimes also their riding horses, consignments of money and so forth.

Costly perfumed gloves were very fashionable and were often used as gifts. An English lord presented Queen Elizabeth with a pair he had brought back from Florence and Catherine de Médicis introduced them to France. In Milan, glove-makers and perfume-makers belonged to the same guild. To reduce the excessive use of gloves and perfume Alessandro Piccolomini suggested that "though noblewomen should wear costly gloves, they should not use any perfume on their persons."

In the Renaissance the interest generally taken in fashion surpassed that of nearly all other periods. Not the women alone, but also the men thought their clothes to be highly important. Two burghers of Augsburg for instance, the Fuggers' accountants Matthaeus and Veit Konrad Schwarz (father and son), had their portraits made in each new garment, and they collected these pictures in their *Klaidungsbuechlein* (Booklet of Garments), specially made for this purpose. Attention was paid not only to the fashion of one's own country, but also to what was worn abroad, of which artists made sketches on their travels; the foreign garments were then often copied at home. Special books recording national costumes were compiled, showing the different garments for each rank in various towns, districts and countries, even including those of the then recently discovered regions outside Europe. For in spite of the fact that they had much in common, the cut of the garments showed many marked peculiarities in the shape of the décolletage or the sleeves and particularly with regard to the fashionable trimmings and the fanciful bonnets and berets, which formed part of the women's everyday dress. Longing for change, people were susceptible to any new thing, and complaints could be heard everywhere about the imitation of foreign costumes. In France there prevailed such an enthusiasm for the fashions of the leading ladies of Italy that Francis I asked Isabella d'Este for a doll dressed like herself, "with the upper and undergarments and the sleeves—as these were often attached only loosely with ribbons—and with her coiffure, so that the ladies at his court could adorn themselves in the same manner." In Italy, on the other hand, clothes after the German, French and, in particular, after the Spanish fashion, seemed worth mentioning. Isabella d'Este exchanged letters with many foreign princesses in which mutual suggestions were made concerning fashions. It was not unusual for these to serve as opportunities for compliments and declarations of sympathy, which were also important for politics. The Queen of Poland asserted that Isabella was the "origin and source of all elegance."

After the mid-sixteenth century the severe and stiff fashion of the Spanish court spread to all countries and superseded even in northern Europe the markedly burghers' costumes of the period of the Reformation. Gala dresses of gold-brocade were introduced, so heavy that the delicate ladies almost succumbed under them. Spanish princesses had sometimes to be carried to the altar as their stiff wedding robes made it impossible for them to walk.

Paintings and graphic works of all kinds can give us an idea of the variety and the changes of fashion in these decades. The people shown in the formal portraits of that period had to be represented according to their rank and therefore always wore their best robes and all their jewelry. But also the pictures of religious themes exhibit the contemporary costume in full detail. Many an engraving of the later 15th or the early 16th century showing an allegorical or biblical figure could almost serve for a fashion plate. Nor is there any lack of reproductions of foolish fashions which look to us like caricatures. The greatest artists made proper costume studies. Holbein drew ladies of the nobility and of the bourgeoisie of Basle in their everyday and in their festive costumes; Dürer depicted the woman of Nuremberg in her workaday dress, her dance-frock and in the robe for her church-going, and he contrasted her plain burgher's costume with that of the smart Venetian lady whose low-necked dresses he repeatedly sketched. On his journey to the Netherlands he made drawings of two Netherlandish garments and a copy of the coat of a Dutch beguine as if for a sewing pattern.

Most striking in the paintings are the costly fabrics used for the garments: the finest cloth, velvet, silk and brocade with patterns in many colours, as well as the great amount of jewelry of gold and precious stones. It is therefore not surprising that this luxury, which was not restricted to court circles but had spread to the bourgeoisie, again and again brought about new regulations, trying to limit the expenditure on clothing accordin to each person's rank. Strict rules as to the material to be used stressed at once the difference of rank in everybody's appearance, and were responsible for creating a great many dissimilarities among the inhabitants of each town. Laws of this kind had been known since the late 14th century but, like those against luxury, became more numerous and more detailed in the 16th. In Germany an imperial clothing order of 1530 fixed the number of the pleats which the skirts of the peasant women in the country, the lowest social order, were allowed to have. But also for the women of the different ranks of the civic population there were rules for the price of their rings, the width of their belts and for the

material of which their hair ribbons had to be made. There were certain restrictions as to the use of velvet and silk by the burgher woman; satin and damask were reserved for the nobility.

In Florence, however, the wives and daughters of the patricians wore the heavy brocades, velvet and silk fabrics with their abundance of patterns manufactured in the town itself and exported to many countries. A great variety of gay contrasting colours was characteristic of the Early Renaissance, fabrics with large patterns were popular. Often the shape of pomegranates was used as a model for these patterns, but there were other models of patterns, some even sketched by famous artists. Motifs always used by the same family became its distinguishing mark; other motifs contained unknown symbols, and to interpret these was a popular party-game.

After the High Renaissance, softer shades were preferred forming harmonious combinations, and the above-mentioned Piccolomini cautions, in his *Dialogue*, the "young woman not to show too many colours in her clothes, in particular not those which do not match well as green and yellow or red and light blue or some other combinations to be found in flags, as such mixtures are not at all refined." At the contemporary courts in other countries fabrics showing sumptuous designs frequently in crude colours, were still the rule, as the colourful costume of the mercenary soldier tended to influence the fashion of the ladies' clothes. The women took over from the men's costume the use of slashes in the upper garment, which displayed the underlying shirt, the undergarment or other differently coloured materials.

The contemporary burgher woman wore as a rule dresses of black cloth, decorated with velvet or silk braids and edged with fur; often there was as a further ornament a broad belt interwoven with gold and silver and trimmed with pearls and precious stones. To the tight bodice belonged a wide, gathered skirt reaching down to the ankles; the shape of the sleeves varied and so did that of the décolleté. Although in some towns, especially in southern Germany, the round, fairly low-neck décolletage—usual in the circles of the nobility—was quite well known, yet high-neck dresses were more often seen; sometimes white shirts were fitted into those with a low neck. Probably as a reaction against the very low-cut décolletage of the late Gothic period, a very severe and simple style was developed under the influence of the Reformation; it was a style which fitted the ideal of the chaste and obedient maiden and of the virtuous house-wife and mother.

A long, usually white, apron was worn over the dress and at the side hung from the belt a bundle of keys, a small case of cutlery, scissors and other like tools, as symbols of the housewife's duties. The women were even portrayed with these insignia of their housewifely might, and the apron, turned into a fancy apron, was accepted by the women of the nobility as part of their costume. The peasant woman and the artisan maids wore similar garments, but simplified and of coarser material, usually with a broad cape-like collar; bodice, skirt and apron were of bright contrasting colours. For the peasant women the German clothing order of 1530 allowed, for reasons of expediency, that the skirts of the workaday clothes might be somewhat shorter, reaching only half-way down the calf of the leg; for the servants this was sometimes even stipulated.

Characteristic of the Renaissance were broad shoes called *Kuhmaul* (cow's mouth), and others decorated with slits called *Bärentatze* (bear's paw); they also super-seded in women's fashions the excessively pointed shoe of the later Gothic period. Moreover there were, especially in Venice, the popular high-heeled shoes, and those on high socles which were sometimes of consider-able height. At first a practical device to avoid the filth of the streets, they were turned into part of the ladies' decorative and fashionable dress, although tall women preferred to do without them.

To complete the dress there were, as already men-tioned, perfumed gloves made of very fine leather; even burgher-women followed this fashion and were often portrayed holding gloves in their hands. The ladies of the higher circles of society usually owned several pairs; Isabella d'Este ordered fourteen pairs of Spanish leather at one time from Rome. In Germany preference was given to buckskin, but the most costly gloves were made of the flexible skin of unborn calves. To restrict the luxury practised in this manner, Cosimo I, Grand Duke of Florence, eventually forbade the ladies to own more than one pair worth ten *scudi*.

Other fashionable accessories were the scarf embroi-dered and trimmed with lace, and the fan, in Italy shaped like a small flag, otherwise usually made of ostrich feathers.

A regular part of the women's outfit was the head-gear, at that time turned into a headdress of many variants. The plain kerchief had gradually, at the late Gothic period, changed into a bonnet of many different shapes; as far as married women were concerned it covered the hair almost completely, and this was put up in plaits under it. At the period of the Renaissance there were pleated and starched bonnets for festive occasions and more simple ones for workdays. The young girls were allowed to wear smaller caps, which displayed the put-up plaits or curls at the temples. Eventually the barret was taken over from the men's fashion; as a quite original headdress, it made its way in the circles of the nobility, and richly decorated with ostrich feathers, it became a fashionable symbol of aristocratic rank. These often enormous constructions were worn dashingly over one ear; to keep them in position they had sometimes to be fastened—as was done by men—on a tight cap worn under them, which was called "calotte." Peasant women had permission to wear only practical hats or caps, which could protect them from the sun. Yet regulations like these often proved useless; every social class transgressed the prohibitions, and peasant women were seen at work dressed in the fashionable costume of the townswoman, with slit sleeves and feathers on a perky barret.

In the Latin countries, probably owing to the warmer climate, the severe and unsophisticated fashion of bon-nets covering all the hair was less popular, and head-gear resembling a scarf was generally worn only by women of the lower ranks. In Italy, in the first half of the 15th century, the hair was worn tightly combed back and then pinned high up and topped by a bonnet shaped like a balloon. Later on preference was given even in court circles to small caps covering the ears, which can be seen in the frescoes of the Palazzo Schifanoia. (Ill. 42) Twelve bonnets and three barrets formed part of the dowry of a Florentine artisan's wife in the second half of the 15th century (38).

Since that time, and specially in the period of the High Renaissance, the Italian women usually wore their hair uncovered; as a rule they still pinned it high up, and instead of covering it with a bonnet, decorated it artistically with veils or ribbons using false hair as well. Sometimes they wore the hair in thick tresses plaited with coloured ribbons, but this was rather exceptional. In the 16th century unplaited hair of shoulder-length also became fashionable; it was usually held together by hairnets, which were popular everywhere. Occasion-

34

ally these nets were very costly, made of thin gold and silver threads and decorated with pearls and precious stones; there were also net-like arrangements of velvet ribbons. In Venice the women wore their hair in a puff over their forehead; this coiffure was so different from the lank hair tightly combed back, which was fashionable everywhere else, that it amazed all strangers when they came to Venice. Casola, the priest from Milan mentioned above, noted in his diary of 1494: "Concerning their coiffure, they wear their hair puffed out so far over their eyes that at first sight they look more like men than women."

A striking characteristic of all Renaissance portraits of women is the exceedingly profuse quantity of jewelry. As the women, like everyone else, were anxious to demonstrate how wealthy they were, they put on all their chains, bracelets and rings. In particular the ingenuous German burgher women were fond of putting one ring on top of another when they were portrayed—sometimes four or five rings on each finger. Rings for which there was no more room on the hands were worn tied to the necklace.

Never before and never afterwards has the expenditure for rings reached such dimensions. Young girls usually wore only one ring, as it was the husband who supplied the mistress of his house with rings for the wedding or during their married life. Bracelets were not so much in use and formed only part of the jewelry of noblewomen; they were made as plain circlets or were formed of interlocked links and worn on top of the long sleeves which often fell down over the back of the hand.

More varied was the shape of the necklaces, made of golden links or of beads. Pendants of all kinds and sizes were extremely popular. Precious stones ingeniously mounted by goldsmiths, or medallions showing gold or silver figures, vied with the embroidered braids, often decorated with pearls, with which the décolletage and the sleeves were trimmed. As with rings, several necklaces were worn on top of one another. Added to this were the ornaments for the hair, made of pearls, stones or precious metals. In the Early Renaissance plain strings of pearls were used to decorate the high foreheads of the Italian women; in the 16th century the headdresses of princesses often consisted of arrangements of artificial blossoms made of precious metals.

THE PRACTICE OF ART

At the time of the Renaissance the women of all countries generally took quite an active part in the practice of art, in particular of music, which was highly valued and formed an important component of the social life of all ranks. Singing and string music were mentioned at all entertainments and soon the first keyboard instruments were added, the clavichord and the English virginal, the painted and carved predecessor of the later spinet. Numerous paintings give us an idea of what these musical entertainments in the circle of friends or the family were like, where the women participating always played the most important role. In pictures of family scenes the wife and daughter usually play the instruments and also in groups of singers the ladies quite often form the centre, as they were evidently able to read music. Musical instruments were frequently added to persons portrayed individually to show that they were versed in the art. Music formed part even of school teaching and in court circles dancing and music were regularly included in the education of girls. It is, however, not known whether any women were professionally engaged in music.

Dancing was one of the most important entertainments in the family circle as well as at public festivities. The rage for dancing in the late middle ages persisted into the Renaissance until the Protestant preachers, especially the Calvinists, protested against it. They forbade chiefly dancing in couples, where men and women hold each other closely; the traditional round dances could resist any change. The dances in the Latin countries were more elaborate than anywhere else. At a dance in Lucca, given by Montaigne, a woman is said to have danced with a cup full of water on her head without spilling a drop. Italian dance-masters were invited to France, where they introduced the Welsh dances, which spread everywhere in the 16th century. The Humanist Vives declaimed against the love of dancing among the ladies of Spanish society: "What use is this immoderate jumping of the girls, whose cavaliers have to support them, holding them by the arms so that they can take a long start, as each of them tries to jump higher than the other?" He turned especially against the fashion of kissing in the course of the dance, which had started in Italy and then spread to France: "What is the use of all this kissing? What pleasure can it be to tire oneself out with jumping all through the night, as if one never could get enough of it. Bad morals have insinuated

Paula Gonzaga Portrayed while Reading

36

themselves now that one may kiss indiscriminately everywhere under the pretext of dancing." (30)

An amateur practice of poetry was, with few exceptions, confined to the higher circles of society. In the regions where the Reformation had been successful some women wrote religious songs; in the Latin countries many learned women are known for their literary endeavours. Some of their works have been preserved and form part of the history of literature.

Early instances are the famous sonnets and improvisations of Cassandra Fedele, who lived at Venice in the 15th century; as well as those of Veronica Gambara, Coreggio's ruler and of Constanze Varano. Vittoria Colonna, 1492—1547, of the noble Roman family of the Colonna, is still well-known today not only for the friendship she entertained in her later years with Michelangelo, but also for her literary work. Her lyrical writings, based on Petrarch's, include love poems addressed to her prematurely deceased husband and, from a later period chiefly religious poetry. Gaspara Stampa, 1523—1554, of a distinguished patrician family, must be mentioned beside Vittoria Colonna; her passionate verses, based on events of her own life, belong to the most beautiful poetry of her time. In Spain there was Caterina Ribera, the author of religious poems and of secular love-songs; she was moreover professor of rhetoric at Salamanca and Alcala.

The women poets of the French Renaissance were as famous as their Italian contemporaries. The literary work of Margaret of Navarre, 1492—1549, sister of Francis I, included religious, lyrical and dramatic works as well as prose writings. Her religious and her secular plays were performed on the amateur stage at a convent which she herself had founded and to which she retired with her ladies-in-waiting, to live there in the refined manner of the Renaissance. Her *Heptameron* is still read today; it is a collection of tales in the manner of Boccaccio, critically and humourously describing the weaknesses of her fellow creatures. A party of noblemen and ladies travelling together recount the tales in the course of seven days; they are frivolous and coarse, as was popular at that time. Some of the travellers represent under the cover of a pseudonym the author's nearest relatives. Then follow discussions among them, chiefly about the relationship between man and woman. The royal author's leading idea was the problem of perfect love, the striving for moral perfection according to Platonic concepts. Side by side with her literary aspirations went her practical economic abilities in running her large household, documented by her accounts and inventories.

The lively intellectual and literary life of France in the first half of the 16th century was not limited to the court. Strongly influenced by Italian Neo-Platonism a school of poets was formed in the old merchants' town of Lyon, which then branched out all over France; women of the bourgeoisie played an outstanding role in it. Pernette du Guillet, who died in 1544, left a volume of *Rimes* (Verses), which shows a close connection with Platonism. In these love poems man appears chiefly as the intellectual guide and model of woman.

Ten years later Louise Labé, 1525—1566, called the "lovely rope-maker," won herself a name as a poet and became a kind of pioneer for the intellectual equality of women and for an unconventional and free style of life. The wife of the well-to-do owner of a rope-making workshop, she kept open house for a circle of the best poets and humanists, and wrote verses which she herself set to music and recited. Best known and repeatedly translated into English are her lovely twenty-four sonnets modelled on those of Petrarch. They treat of her experience of unrequited love. A psychologically well-founded prose dialogue between foolishness and love shows her to have been well versed in antiquity.

Sonnet XXII

Luisant Soleil, que tu es bien heureus
De voir tousiours de t'Amie la face:
Et toy, sa seur, qu'Endimion embrasse,
Tant te rapais de miel amoureus.

Mars voit Venus: Mercur aventureus
De Ciel en Ciel, de lieu en lieu se glasse.
Et Jupiter remarque en mainte place
Ses premiers ans plus gays et chaleureus.

Voila du Ciel la puissante harmonie,
Qui les esprits divins ensemble lie;
Mais s'ils avoient ce qu'ils ayment lointein,

Leur harmonie et ordre irrevocable
Se tourneroit en erreur variable,
Et comme moy travailleroient en vain.

Resplendent Sun, how happy is your lot
Who daily gaze on your beloved's face:
And you who taste Endymion's embrace,
Sweet moon, can nightly find him in his grot.

Mars can see Venus; Mercury can plot
A course from heaven to heaven for his chase:
And Jupiter can see in many a place
The pledges of his love in youth begot.

Such is the harmony which rules the skies
And links together these divinities.
But if their loves were absent from their sight

Their heavenly order could no longer reign,
But all would turn to chaos and foul night
And all their toil, like mine, would be in vain.

Besides her there were quite a number of ladies of the merchant's class dominating the social life and its literary circles. Nor were they inferior to their Italian models with regard to their personal appearance; clever dressmakers copied for them garments in the most recent Italian fashion.

In Poitiers, Madeleine des Roches and her daughter Catherine became known as poets. Catherine upheld the right of women to culture and learning. From men, however, voices could be heard at the same time which condemned the women's striving for education and their interest in art, or conceded this only to ladies of high rank. Jean Bouchet wrote: "Some people found it unusual for a lady to use her brains to think out books, but this is thoughtless, because to be able to join in the discussion one has first to distinguish and to find out of what kind of family the ladies are, whether they are poor or rich. I am of the opinion that women from the more common ranks, who are compelled to care for simple domestic duties, ought not to venture into art, as this is contrary to their homely character. But queens, princesses and other ladies who, out of regard for their rank have not to trouble themselves about household matters, should fill their minds with the study of the arts and dedicate their leisure to good and virtuous knowledge, which leads to noble things, polite manners and perfection and not to dancing, jollification or banquets." (30)

Many lady amateurs of these circles therefore took up poetry. For instance one spoke highly of the literary gifts of the young Mary Stuart while she lived in France at the court of the Valois, married almost as a child to Francis II, who was also not of age. The poet Brantome reported of her: "She spoke in a very dainty and sweet manner and had a nimble way of writing poetry, for I saw her often retire to her room and return at once to show verses thought out that very moment." (30)

Nor is it from Italy alone but also from countries north of the Alps that the names are known of quite a number of women artists of the 16th century, who practised painting not as a hobby but professionally; yet only a few of their works can today be identified with certainty. The strict regulations of the guilds in the German towns allowed the women only subordinate activity in the trades and crafts. Nor could they do any independent work in the arts ruled by the guilds, still fewer gained there the title of master; yet it seems likely that a certain amount of what was produced in the artists' workshops was the work of women, of the master's wife or daughter. A document from Cracow, dated 1538, mentions a Polish artist, Dorothea Baczkowska. Albrecht Dürer speaks, in the diary of his journey to the Netherlands, of Susanna, the eighteen-year-old daughter of Geraert Horebolt, the artist of altar-pieces and miniatures in Ghent. He thought her so good at drawing, a "great miracle," that he paid a florin for a sheet from her hand with a picture of Christ. Most likely her work was completely mixed up with the other products of the workshop, so that nothing has been preserved carrying her name. Lost also are the works of other Netherlandish women artists famous at their time, for instance, those of Marie Bessemer, 1520—1560, known as Mayken Verhulst, the grandmother and earliest teacher of Jan Brueghel, later called "Velvet Brueghel." The same applies to Lievine Bening, whom King Henry VIII summoned to London and who then lived as a celebrated portraitist at the English court. She is said to have preferred small-sized work, as did also other Netherlandish women artists, who applied themselves chiefly to miniatures, but of whom the names only are known.

Several works have been preserved by the portraitist Catharina van Hemessen of Antwerp, the daughter of the well-known artist Jan van Hemessen; they are dated and signed with her full name. Later she and her husband followed Queen Mary of Hungary to Spain when she had abdicated as stadholder of the Netherlands. Catharina van Hemessen's self-portrait of 1548 shows her working at the easel; it is a charming picture, faithfully and naively painted, of a rather shy young burgher's daughter, who was nevertheless self-confident enough to choose for her work the then fairly uncommon subject of a portrait of herself at work.

In Italy a wider scope was given to artistic work, and women artists could work independently outside their father's workshops and seriously compete with their male colleagues. The humanistic education established there the prerequisite for the pursuit of art, not necessarily arising from an artisan's family tradition. A good example is the patrician family Anguisciola of Cremona, of whom all six daughters were artists. The works of Sofonisba, the eldest daughter, born in 1527, became famous in her lifetime. In 1559 Philipp II summoned her to the court of Spain; according to Vasari she lived there with the Queen, drew a considerable salary, and was stared at in wonder by all the court. Vasari specially mentions one of her drawings, which he included in his own renowned collection of free-hand drawings. With respect to her, versed also in music and all humanities, he even quoted a verse from Ariosto's *Orlando Furioso*: "Women have gained great fame in any art to which they turned." Van Dyck visited the artist when she was ninety-six and had gone blind; he afterwards said he had never learned so much about painting in so short a time from any human being as from her. Several of her works, some self-portraits, a double portrait of herself and her husband, and another of three of her sisters playing chess, hang beside paintings of her male contemporaries in museums and art galleries all over the world.

The gifted Irena di Spilembergo who died at the age of nineteen is also worth mentioning. Titian himself had been her teacher. Furthermore there was also the daughter of Tintoretto, who died young and of whom self-portraits are extant. Lavinia Fontana, the daughter and disciple of a Bolognese artist, was celebrated as the fashionable portraitist of the Roman nobility. She was summoned to Rome under Pope Clement VIII, and not only portrayed ladies of the nobility but also tried her hand at historical subjects. Her wealthy husband, who was an amateur artist, is said to have sometimes finished off the garments in her pictures. Not less well known was Artemisia Gentileschi, who worked in England as a portraitist but was also able to paint large pictures with religious themes and to accept commissions for monumental work.

Finally there was the work of Properzia de Rossi, noteworthy as that of one of the earliest women sculptors. According to Vasari minutely carved work in small pieces of material was her speciality, the kind of work treasured in the curio cabinets of the Mannerist period, like the popular carved peach stones; the Italian artist is said to have carved on such stones scenes of the Passion, each showing a number of figures. She also applied simultaneously, through her husband, for monumental work in marble for the Church of San Petronio in Bologna, her native town. A marble portrait, which she had submitted for trial, was approved, she was assigned the task and performed it satisfactorily. (Ill. 82)

At the courts all artistic activities were probably never more than hobbies for the ladies. Only as patrons or as collectors have many women of princely rank at the period of the Renaissance gained lasting fame in the south as well as in the north. In these roles they also considerably influenced contemporary art.

Conspicuous among the Italian courts was Mantua, again thanks to Isabella d'Este, who was known as a passionate collector, always greedy to acquire works of art, and quite unscrupulous in obtaining them even from friends or relatives. She shared the contemporary enthusiasm for all things from antiquity, employed agents to procure coins, vases and sculptures, and bought Netherlandish masters of the 15th century, then much sought after by Italian art-lovers, among them a Jan van Eyck; but she was just as eager to collect works of contemporary Italian art. She was not satisfied with the works of artists working at Mantua, but ordered others from the most famous masters through the mediation of her numerous influential friends. She had always quite definite requests and ideas, with which at that time the artists were not always very willing to agree. Thus she asked in vain for a painting by Leonardo da Vinci, which was to show Jesus in the temple before the Pharisees and scribes, and she asked for "a young Christ with that expression of charm and gentleness, which you know so well to depict." For the allegorical pictures, which she valued greatly, she laid down for the artist not only subject and size, but gave exact instructions as to the number, the arrangement and the garments of the figures to be shown, and even provided small sketches for them. Lorenzo Costa's *Court of the Muses*, where she was shown as queen in the realm of poets, was made in this manner. Isabella was so pleased with the result that she offered the artist the post of court painter.

At the same time Margaret of Austria, the Stadholder of the Netherlands, had begun a large collection of paintings at her residence at Mechlin. This collection was the first of its kind north of the Alps, then unique in its importance to art. Inventories reveal the large number of works by the earlier Netherlandish artists included in the collection, such as Jan van Eyck, Hieronymus Bosch, Rogier van der Weyden, Hans Memling and Dirk Bouts; moreover there were included antique and modern bronzes and a great number of valuable illuminated manuscripts. The stadholder, who herself painted and wrote poetry, attracted many eminent artists to Mechlin and furthered with her commissions the development of Renaissance culture north of the Alps. Conrad Meit from Worms was her court sculptor; his chief works were made for her, notably the three magnificent marble tombs at Brou in the south of France, for Margaret herself, her mother, and her prematurely deceased husband. Two small busts of boxwood, which show Margaret wearing a pleated bonnet are also by Conrad Meit; here she looks more like a simple burgher's housewife than like the energetic ruler that she was, equally well versed in politics, learning and art. Among the painters whom she valued in particular was Jacopo de Barberi; she was unwilling to let Albrecht Dürer have his sketch-book when she personally showed him her collections. Dürer recorded this visit to "Frau Margarethe" in the diary of his journey to the Netherlands in 1521.

Of the art-loving women at other European courts Isabella of Castile, 1451—1504, deserves mentioning: her portraits by Rogier van der Weyden, Dirk Bouts and Hans Memling later came into the sepulchral chapel of the two "Catholic Kings" in the Cathedral of Granada where they still are today. Mary of Hungary bequeathed her collection to her art-loving nephew Philipp II, whereby Rogier van der Weyden's famous early painting, the *Descent from the Cross*, came to Spain.

France owes at least one still extant inventory of a collection of that period, to a woman's assiduity and interest in art: Michele Gaillard of Longemueau, the wife of the minister Florimond Robertet, wrote with her own hand in 1532, at Bury, a list of the works of art which had belonged to her late husband. According to a contemporary (Bandello) a strange kind of collection was established by Maria Verré, a lady at Antwerp: she had all her admirers painted by famous artists. (30)

WORK AND PUBLIC ACTIVITIES

The Bell-Caster

As compared with the middle ages the independent professional activities of women were more and more restricted in the Renaissance. In the 14th century, women had still been able to reach a position of equality with men in the guilds, from the late 15th century they were gradually excluded from them. The increased competition due to the economic crisis at the end of the middle ages required new and stricter guild regulations; through these the women were shut out from the trades and frequently even their participation in commerce was limited. The wife was, however, still looked upon as her husband's assistant and had therefore to perform certain duties connected with his trade or craft—this besides her own special duties in kitchen and household. The professions not controlled by the guilds and the nursing of the sick, on behalf of the city or the Church, offered her a chance of some, if limited, work.

Among the peasant population in the country, men and women of course went on working together as has been done at all times. The part of the peasants' work performed by women is recorded in numerous pictures, especially the illustrations in the calendars, which were already in use in the middle ages and were popular also in the 15th and 16th centuries. The pictures for the individual months showed the work characteristic of each of them, and as that work—sowing, reaping and the breeding of the farm animals—had for centuries hardly ever changed, these pictures, too, permanently repeated the same motifs. In the field the men did the heavier work, mowing, loading, ploughing, while the women's duty was the tying of sheaves, the turning of the hay and other similar additional occupations, especially at harvest time, but they are sometimes also seen holding a sickle. The wearisome work of dressing the flax was mostly done by women who had of course also to attend to all the additional work, the spinning and weaving. Of the work connected with the breeding of farm animals, the milking and churning were the women's concern, while all members of the family helped with the shearing of the sheep, the harvesting and treading the grapes. The early "slaughter feast" brought special work for the peasant woman and her maids, as they had to look after the preparation of the meat and the making of the sausages. The farm products were taken to the markets in town by the peasant woman together with her husband; she is often depicted on this traditional errand, with the egg basket on her head or hanging from her arm, and carrying the dead poultry in her hand.

The activities of the artisan's wife in the towns were manifold. The apprentices and the journeymen lived in the master's house and his wife had to feed them and often ruled over them quite severely. Usually the sale of her husband's wares was included in the list of her duties which was fixed by the statutes of the guilds. In the pictures of the artisan's life the wife is seen sitting at the distaff in the workshop, looking after the children, so as to be ready any moment, if necessary, to serve the customers, either in the workshop itself or through a window to the street. Like the peasants' the artisans' wives sold the goods in the booths of the market. As did the wives of all other artists, Agnes, Dürer's wife, sold the sheets with the graphic work of her husband in the markets of Nuremberg.

Of the chief work in the artisan's workshop only the rudimentary and subsidiary part was done by the women of the family, as they were excluded from learning a trade. In the 16th century the rules of the guilds in nearly all trades forbade the women to become apprentices or to sit for any examinations which might have enabled them to become journeymen or masters; only exceptionally was a widow allowed to run her late husband's business until her son could take over; the statutes of each guild contained special regulations for this. Some of the guild regulations fixed also the kind of help which women were allowed to give: it was forbidden to keep any maids specially for the workshop; only the housemaids, when they had finished with their housework, were permitted to give some simple manual help, which could not be connected with the workshop's trade proper; they could, for example, poke the fire.

Some specially feminine work, forming part of the making of textile materials, for instance the spinning and weaving of silk, had in the middle ages been done mainly in convents. In the 13th and 14th centuries it was also done by guild-regulated trades, where it was predominantly the work of women, who carried it out under the supervision of women masters. In the 16th century all this work was also put into the hands of men. A large number of women had thereby lost their economic independence. Only as hired workers could they now make their living by taking up one or other newly-established trade, such as for example the making of pillow lace. It had

not been found possible to do without the help of the women's deft fingers for this delicate work.

This new technique of lace-making had started at Venice and then spread quickly over Europe, furthered by an increased longing for finery in the 15th century. It became a favourite occupation for women and girls of the upper classes. For them a large number of books was published with models and sketches for lace-making and embroidery, usually designed by men. One book of this kind, published in Italy in 1530, is called *Modelbook from which tender young maidens and noblewomen may learn all the finesse which a virtuous woman may employ with the needle in her hand in honour of this book.* Lace-making served, however, not only for the "usage and entertainment of noble ladies and maidens," as is indicated by the title of another modelbook, but became in the course of the 16th century, in several countries, a home industry mostly in the hands of women and as such an important source of income for them. In Normandy the fishers' wives and girls made pillow lace; Valenciennes in France and Mechlin (Malines) in the Netherlands were turned into centres for fine bobbin work, while the lace of Brussels attained its greatest fame in the 17th century.

In Germany, Barbara Uttmann, the wife of a wealthy owner of mines at Annaberg, introduced the making of pillow lace in the Saxon Erzgebirge. In approximately 1560, when mining fast began to decline there, this delicate needlework offered the women and young girls a means of earning a livelihood; associated with the weaving of braids, it gradually developed in these regions also into the most important branch of home industry. After her husband's death the energetic and efficient Barbara Uttmann took over his mining business, and also organized the women's work; she eventually became the head of a big enterprise, employing nine hundred women lace-workers. Other women of the leading Annaberg families followed her example and organized the sale of lace made in large quantities by wage-earners from the poorer layers of the population. Brave and enterprising, they undertook this big business as would merchants.

In other branches of commerce, as well, women were able to rely on themselves and to work independently. The women of merchants' families often partook actively, or at least as silent partners, in the big commercial or financial enterprises. The legal equality which women had enjoyed in commerce in the late 13th cen-

*Women Buying
from a Hawker Displaying
his Goods on a Tray*

tury had been preserved to a great extent, and enabled them to conclude independent business transactions. Daughters and widows of rich merchants profitably invested their capital in textiles and other enterprises. Frequent representations by Netherlandish artists of tax-collectors or money-changers, with their wives standing as assistants beside them, show that the wife joined in her husband's business. She followed up her husband's activities and was herself occupied counting and weighing the money, keeping account books, or in direct negotiations. An Italian traveller described the impression he had gained of the women in the Netherlands in 1518 in the following words: "They are so efficient that they can give directions, keep the accounts and do everything. Men and women are active in the same way with regard to buying in the open market, to selling, and in the public practice of all trades." (45)

The participation of women in the retail trade, and in the guilds of the hucksters and costermongers was especially large. In contrast to the guild of the artisans, these guilds conceded independent rights to married women and accepted as members single women, who earned their living by selling foodstuffs and other commodities for everyday use or by trading in second-hand goods. Wherever such independent activities were available, they became tempting to many daughters of the lower ranks of the civic population; a decree of Dresden of the year 1604 complained that they preferred to become hucksters than to serve as hardworked maids. (45) There were, however, isolated cases even of guilds for retail trade limiting the activities of women; in some towns, for instance, the wives of salt merchants were allowed to take over their husband's business in the market only when he was ill.

Midwives and teachers did not belong to any guilds. Certified midwives, paid by the city, were already known in the 16th century. Experienced midwives of mature age trained the apprentices and doctors instructed them, although without themselves ever practising obstetrics. A regulation of Strasbourg dated 1556 stipulated that women applying for the honoured post of a sworn-in midwife had to pass an examination conducted by the city doctor in the presence of some respected and experienced women burghers, appointed by the city council.

As had already been the case in the middle ages, the teaching of girls in schools was almost exclusively in the hands of women. Nuns taught in the convents, and so-called "school-women" taught in the girls' schools which were established in many towns from the 15th century. At first these women used to be the wives of the schoolmasters appointed to teach the boys. In the course of the Reformation the civic authorities endeavoured to employ as schoolmistresses former nuns who had accepted the new faith. They had to teach an elementary knowledge of reading and writing, sometimes also of music; they were equal to their male colleagues in respect of general consideration and probably also as to their salary.

Unmarried women, who found a home in the convents, could teach young girls there or nurse the sick. The daughters of families of lesser means—unless they became servants—joined one of the half religious, half secular communities, such as the Beguines or the *Schwestern vom gemeinsamen Leben* (Sisters of Joint Life). Originally charitable work and the nursing of the poor and the sick had been the main task of these institutions. But at the time of their decline in the 15th and 16th centuries their inmates had sometimes to earn their living by artisans' work, although the guilds always remonstrated against it. When in the course of the Reformation many convents and similar institutions had been dissolved, the care of the poor and the sick continued, as a rule, to constitute mainly a domain of women's activities. Reputable women undertook, either for a salary or as honorary work, the nursing of the inmates of hospitals or homes for incurables supported by the city or the Church or by private donations.

The activities of the ladies of noble rank were more limited than those of the women of the bourgeoisie. Their education provided only for matrimony with men of equal status, which required just enough knowledge of domestic work to enable them to give orders to the kitchen staff and to do some needlework as a pastime of their own.

Some women of the reigning European dynasties achieved importance in history through their political activities. Splendour and fame, yet sometimes also blood and terror, are attached to the names of these princesses and queens, who represent the female counterpart of the man of the Renaissance, equally outstanding through energy, intelligence and unscrupulous character. They often combined a degree of courage which one almost feels should be the prerogative of man, combining diplomatic skill with a woman's refinement. The number of outstanding events in history which are connected with the name of a woman is therefore larger in the 16th century than at any other period.

First of all must be mentioned Queen Elizabeth of England, whose reign (1558—1603) is known in history

Nursing

as the Elizabethan Age. Under her rule, England rose rapidly to the position of the most powerful seafaring nation in Europe, while poetry—Shakespeare—and music also flourished. Before her another woman had occupied the throne of England, her step-sister Mary Tudor, whose short reign from 1553 to 1558 is remembered in history under the infamous name of "Bloody Mary." Her efforts for the Catholic religion led her to persecute with fire and sword all suspect heretics, at that time mainly Lutheran Protestants. Elizabeth on the other hand, trying to secure the religious unity of the country, favoured the reintroduction of Protestantism, until eventually Anglicanism became the official religion of the country. The Queen furthered the economic power of the country by supporting first of all the merchant class; the Stahlhof, the London office of the German Hansa, was closed in 1598; the Stock Exchange was founded in London. The cancellation of the prohibition to export grain gave an important impetus to agriculture, so that a contemporary could report the English peasants to be more proudly attired than the noblemen in Germany. In foreign affairs, Elizabeth backed the Netherlands with money and arms in their fight against Spain. The victory over the Spanish Armada finally secured for England the complete control of the seas. The first English colony, founded in 1607 on the other side of the ocean, was called Virginia in honour of the unmarried queen.

The conflict between Elizabeth and Mary Stuart was mainly political. The daughter of James V of Scotland looked upon herself as the rightful queen of England, although the last will of Henry VIII had excluded her from the succession. Her complicity in the murder of her second husband increased the manifest hostility of the two queens, which eventually led to Mary's death on the scaffold. This event darkened Elizabeth's fame, and her attitude towards her minions Leicester and Essex was also harshly criticized. The weaknesses of character of this highly cultivated woman have often been put into the foreground by historians.

In France Anne de Beaujeu, 1460—1522, had been regent for her brother, later King Charles VIII, before he became of age. Although still very young herself, she was a skilful ruler, filled all high posts with her relatives or favourites, reduced the state expenditures as well as the taxes, pardoned exiles and freed political prisoners; in 1485 she succeeded in breaking a revolt of the barons by

diplomatic means and force of arms. In spite of the efforts of her enemies she secured the throne for her brother; in 1491 she married him to the Duchess Anne, heiress of Brittany, and then herself retired completely from politics.

Still better known in the history of France, is Catherine de Médicis, 1519—1589, a member of the famous Florentine family. After the death of her husband, King Henry II, she forcibly gained the regency for her second son, Charles IX, and from then on played a decisive role in French politics, at first mediating between the two opposing religious factions. When, however, she saw Coligni, the head of the Huguenots, steadily win more influence over her son, she ordered the leader of the Huguenots, who where assembled in Paris for the wedding of her daughter with Henry of Bourbon and Navarre, to be killed in the "bloodbath of St. Bartholomew."

Among the Spanish queens Isabella I, 1451—1504, gained some importance together with her husband Ferdinand of Aragon. She commissioned the Genoese Christopher Columbus to find a passage by sea to India; on the other hand, her court was the starting point of the Inquisition.

It is significant that the kings of Poland and of Hungary at the time of the Renaissance chose their wives from the princely families of Italy, who then contributed to the dissemination of Italian art and culture in their new countries.

The Netherlands were ruled for three generations by three women greatly gifted in politics. Under their regencies the economic development of the Netherlands reached its peak, but this was also the period of the bitter religious and social struggles, which ended with the liberation of the Dutch provinces from Spanish rule.

The Emperor Maximilian I entrusted his daughter Margaret at her own request with the regency of the Netherlands when she had been widowed for the second time at the age of twenty-five. Her mother, Maximilian's wife Maria, was born a princess of Burgundy, and Margaret grew up at the French court. For her residence as stadholder she chose Mechlin, and there started upon her regency, which was distinguished by more than two decades of economic and diplomatic successes; her nephew, the Emperor Charles V, confirmed her as regent after Maximilian's death. Although she had dedicated her private life to art and poetry, she yet possessed so much clever skill for practical politics that she could disentangle the confused finances of the state and even strengthen them. In external politics she brought about the peace of Cambrai, in German sometimes called "ladies peace" *(Damenfriede)*. It was signed on 15th August 1529 by herself and Louise of Savoy, the skilful and awesome mother of the French king. By this treaty, France gave up her claims on Italy and thereby left her Italian sympathizers to the mercy of the Empire's rule, while Charles V, in exchange, desisted from his claims on Burgundy and set free his enemy's sons whom he had held prisoners. The war-like strife from which both France and Italy had suffered for decades was thus brought to an end through the energetic mediation of two women. There began then in Italy a period of powerful political interference from Spain and the Empire, which put an end to her independence and her cultural leadership.

After Margaret's death Emperor Charles V handed over the regency of the Netherlands to his sister Mary, the widow of the Hungarian King Louis II, who had fallen fighting the invading Turks in the battle of Mohács. She moved her residence to Brussels, her native town. Although with regard to intellectual life and art her court was not as splendid as had been that of Margaret, she nevertheless was a ruler of great political ability, which was acknowledged also by the people. Yet the conflicts between the Netherlands and Spain became serious during her regency. The flourishing commercial centres of Flanders and Holland had to accept Spanish garrisons, and bloodshed followed Charles V's intervention against those of the burghers who had seceded from the Catholic Church. The emperor feared that a Protestant Netherlands could weaken his position with regard to France and the Protestant Estates of the Empire, and he therefore joined the Church in the fight against heretics. The inquisition persecuted alike the Lutherans, Baptists and Calvinists. The revolt of the people finally led to a revolutionary movement which brought about the secession of the Northern Provinces of Holland from Spain.

These events took place under the regency of the third woman stadholder, Margaret of Parma. When Charles V resigned in 1556, Mary of Hungary gave up the regency and retired to Spain. Four years later Philipp II entrusted the regency to his stepsister, who was greatly devoted to him. Margaret of Parma was the illegitimate daughter of Charles V and Johanna van der Gheest, a Flemish patrician from Oudensarde; she was brought up in accordance with her rank and in a strictly Catholic manner in Brussels at the court of Mary of Hungary. Domineering and quick-tempered as she was known to be, but versed on the one hand in the customs of the Dutch people and on the other in the aims of Spanish politics, she endeavoured to check the rise of opposition to Spain by a clever policy of mediation with the Spanish aristocracy, the counts Egmont and Oranien. She obtained the dismissal of Granvilla, who had been associated with her as a state minister and whose influence she feared. But when she herself was eventually asked to hand in her resignation to the Duke of Alba, she gave up her office and retired to Italy.

The women at the courts of northern Italy also showed diplomatic skill. The very same ladies, prominent in cultural and social life, also played an important role in the mutual political intrigues and quarrels of their small principalities and in the war-like strife with France. As representatives of their husbands they governed and organized the economy of their countries, gained advantages for their families and intervened skilfully in high politics. The ideal of the heroic woman of the Renaissance with her manly courage and strength of mind was modelled upon them.

Isabella d'Este has been called a female Machiavelli. When her husband was absent, she ruled in Mantua and worked, firm of purpose and with great skill, for the welfare of the duchy. She took the initiative in establishing in Mantua the manufacture of velvet, satin and damask, as well as of berets, and this soon became the chief source of income for the inhabitants. But her main concern was for the careers of her sons. When the eldest had acceded to the throne, she assisted him as a clever and far-seeing counsellor. So as to procure for one of her younger sons a cardinal's hat, she spent two years in Rome, where she witnessed the *sacco di Roma*, the conquest and sacking of the town by foreign mercenaries. She offered asylum to three thousand people in her palace, which she had fortified in time and provided with arms so that it was one of the few spared by the looting bands.

Amazon-like ladies, too, were known and glorified in the Renaissance. They wore men's attire and fearlessly joined in the battles on horseback. Louise Labé, the poetess from Lyon mentioned above, is said to have dressed at the age of sixteen like a courtly gentleman and, assuming the pseudonym of Captain Loys, to have taken part in the siege of Perpignan in 1542. In Italy the heroic Caterina Sforza was celebrated as a *virago* and given the title of honour of *Prima donna d'Italia*. One spoke simultaneously of the charming and delicate Caterina and of the bloodthirsty "tigress of Forli," who flinched from no cruelty. When Pope Sixtus IV died, she rode to Rome, still a young woman, as her husband's representative, at the head of an army of mercenaries and occupied the Castello S. Angelo by force of arms, in the vain hope of influencing the election of the pope. She showed extreme courage during the events following the murder of her husband Girolamo Riario. Although her enemies threatened to kill her six children, whom they held as hostages, she refused to surrender the castle and thereby saved the rule of the Riario in Forli; afterwards she took terrible revenge in a bath of blood. As guardian of her children she then took over the government of her small state and dedicated herself to its welfare; she proved a prudent and severe ruler.

In times of war, when she rode into battle, Caterina Sforza is said to have worn armour under her garments, but otherwise she led the life of any woman, thinking of nothing but love and beauty. Her castle at Forli was as luxurious as that of any other court and her collection of beauty recipes and drugs proves her to have been an expert in cosmetics. Her little book written by her own hand, called *Experimenti*, contained in code also the recipe for a poison, which was supposed to kill the victim in the course of a month. When her sons had one of her influential and pretentious lovers put to death, she again took dreadful revenge; she ordered even her own children to be taken and imprisoned. As a result she had once more to live through the siege and the conquest of her castle and town. As booty of Cesare Borgia she was led in triumphal procession to Rome. Even her last years, which she spent in Florence, dedicating herself to the education of her youngest son, were filled with constant quarrels, this time with the Medici.

Of still greater, although dubious, fame Lucrezia Borgia, the daughter of Pope Alexander VI has gone down in the history of the Renaissance. Her name is connected with the darkest side of that epoch, the intrigues and murders around the papal court. Yet she herself was only a puppet in the hands of the Borgia and their dynastic interests, especially in those of her ambitious and bloodthirsty brother Cesare. He forced her to conclude marriages advantageous to his political plans.

After he had killed her beloved husband, the twenty-year-old Alfonso of Aragon, Duke of Biseglia, he compelled her to marry Alfonso d'Este, then the hereditary prince of Ferrara; at his side she led, according to contemporary records, a virtuous and exemplary life.

Prominent as an independent personality among the ladies of the German princely courts was Anna of Saxony, 1532—1582, a Danish princess. She was often reproached with interfering in the politics of her husband, the Elector Augustus of Saxony. As she was not any less energetic and active than her husband, he turned over to her the administration of certain domains of his government, horticulture, medicine and art. In questions of politics, too, he liked to listen to the expert opinion of his wife, although he otherwise ruled in a rather patriarchal way. Anna was a strict Lutheran and as such played a major part in the religious politics of the Saxon court. It was at her suggestion that one of the rival Protestant groups, the so-called Philippists, followers of Melanchthon, was banned from the court. Because of her care for the poor and the sick, and the establishment of a court pharmacy, noted above, and of a school for midwives, she was known to the people as "Mother Anna."

The Reformation could repeatedly rely on the active assistance of women. Renata di Francia, 1510—1575, the daughter of King Louis XII of France and wife of Ercole d'Este, supported the Huguenots and turned the strictly Catholic court of Ferrara into an asylum for French emigrants who sided with the Protestants and tried to spread the new faith. Under Calvin's direct influence, the clever Frenchwoman became one of his most eager disciples and followers; by the personal favour of the pope she was granted an exceptional position with regard to the Inquisition. In France itself Margaret of Navarre stood up for the Reformation and the protection of its adherents, though she personally remained faithful to the Roman Catholic religion. The pedantic professors of the Sorbonne therefore accused her of heresy.

Mention must also be made of another active Lutheran in the Saxon districts: Catherine of Mecklenburg, who persuaded her husband, Duke Henry of Freiberg, to accept the tenets of the Reformation.

Pamphlets issued in the service of the Reformation show that burghers' and peasant women were publicly active in the fight for their faith; armed with hay-forks and threshing-flails, they attacked monks and priests. Yet in the social circles of the learned Reformers and at Luther's own table there was no room for such women; Luther did not think much of women for their gift of conversation: "When women are eloquent, that is not praiseworthy; it suits them much better to stammer or to speak badly."

Finally attention must be drawn to the active part played in politics by women of the oppressed classes. In their ranks, too, there were heroic women, who took up arms in the German Peasants' War of the early 16th century; they fought in support of the revolutionary cause sometimes with even more fanaticism and courage than the men. Chronicles mention the part taken by these "housewives," mostly peasants, though some were women from the towns, who placed themselves at the side of the peasants in revolt and went forth with them "with arms and weapons, in shining armour."

One simple woman from Bökingen, a village near Heilbronn, has won herself a place in history as the "Jeanne d'Arc of the Peasants' War." She was known in all the districts around the Neckar as the *Schwarze Hofmännin* (Black Farm Woman); the superstition of the age ascribed to her secret powers, witchcraft and visionary gifts, because she was able to arouse and to enhance enthusiasm in the peasants' army. Already at the very beginning of the social unrest in Heilbronn this woman from a village is said to have mixed with the people of the town and to have fanned their revolt against the town council. Stirred by hatred of the nobles and the patricians in the towns, she joined the band of peasants from the Neckar district led by Jäcklin Rohrbach, and became the adviser of this revolutionary leader of the peasants. She was his equal in energy and firmness, but nursed a special hatred, aimed at the proud patrician women of Heilbronn. She wanted to "cut their clothes from their bodies so that they would have to run about like plucked geese;" the town of Heilbronn should be destroyed, "it ought to be made into a village and everything levelled out." She was in the ranks of the *Heller Haufen* (Bright Band) of 8,000 peasants from the Neckar and the Odenwald when they conquered Weinsberg and gained a victory over the hated Württembergian governor, and she was again with them when subsequently the town of Heilbronn had to surrender and became the centre for various bands of peasants.

WOMEN SLAVES, BEGGARS, WITCHES, COURTESANS AND CONCUBINES

The splendour of civic culture, the development of knowledge and art cannot hide the dark side of the period of the Renaissance: there were two clearly conflicting aspects of that epoch. The economic boom, due to early capitalism, had given rise to new social problems. The plight of the country folk led, in some parts of Germany, to the Peasants' War; a pre-proletarian class of wage-earners was formed in the towns, which contrasted sharply with the wealthy patricians.

In Italy there still lived, in the 15th century, slaves as maids in the houses of the leading families, who with their palaces, with what they did to further art and with the commissions they gave to artists represented the quintessence of Italian Renaissance culture. Every year Venetian ships brought women from foreign countries—as a rule they were of Tartar extraction—and the Italian states as well as the Church suffered them to be sold as housemaids, provided they did not first profess the Christian faith. The patrician women looked upon them as if they were merchandise and chose those who seemed fit for heavy work by their physique and their character; the master of the house and his sons probably considered more the slave's beauty. Slaves who lived up to the expectations of the buyer were treated in the same way as other servants and were sometimes even set free in their old age. If the masters were not satisfied with them, they were beaten or resold. (68)

The worst existence was that of the people who could not earn their living—the sick, the cripples and the destitute old—who could just avert starvation by begging. The charity of the monasteries and convents, civic institutions and private foundations or hospitals were able to relieve only a small part of the misery. The incurable and the infectious sick were not even allowed to live in the community, the cripples and the blind frequently vegetated in complete poverty at the mercy of the people around them. The beggars' regulations, which became more and more frequent in the 16th century, looked upon the begging by the native poor as something quite normal and justifiable; they turned only against intruding outsiders. Pieter Brueghel the Elder painted those poorest of the poor, who were to be seen in the streets of every town and wandered begging through all the country. Among the large numbers of figures in his pictures and among the happy carnival scenes depicted there, one sees emaciated women, who display children and cripples to get a mite from the rich.

The development of science and the expansion of humanistic thought were in the 16th century still partly counteracted by the persistence of mediaeval conceptions; occultism and superstition, astrology and the fear of demons still influenced even educated persons. People practised alchemy to produce gold, but also to mix poisons, and they studied the Cabbala to acquire knowledge of the supernatural. Bianca Capello, the lovely mistress and later wife of the Grand Duke Francesco I of Florence was quite generally accused of being an experienced poisoner; she worked together with the Grand Duke at experiments in his laboratory.

Champions of all religions agreed that magicians, witches and unbelievers had to be persecuted without mercy. In Spain the Inquisition attained to its peak under the Grand Inquisitor Tomás de Torquemada (after 1481), and then also reached the Netherlands. In Germany and in France the persecution centered on the cruel pursuit of women decried as witches. Though it included magicians and sorcerers as well, yet their number was small compared with the very large number of trials of witches who, much more often than the men, were looked upon as tools of Satan.

This unimaginable mass madness was based on the *Malleus maleficarum* (Witches' Hammer), a book written by the inquisitors Heinrich Insistoris and Jakob Sprenger and published in 1489. Each suspicion, each calumny led to a denunciation and this was sufficient to fix the date for a trial. Anyone who did not believe in witches, was himself thought to be a heretic. A natural phenomenon or disaster, an illness or death usually formed the occasion of the accusation of women, until then quite blameless, of dealings with the devil. Whenever suspicion arose, an inquisitorial trial was started; as a rule this ended with a condemnation to death combined with terrible torments. The interrogations usually disclosed the names of yet other witches or "hags," and consequently each trial started off chains of arrests and led to the hearing of more and more witnesses. The protocols of the trials often contain, word by word, mostly absurd statements and confessions extracted by harsh torture. The women were accused of intercourse with the devil, and this was supposed to make them willing to commit any kind of misdeed. In their agony the tortured women put on record that they had destroyed the harvest at the order of the devil, poisoned wells, and killed men and beasts with ointments and potions. A midwife in the town of Dillingen confessed in 1587 to having been responsible, during the many years of her work, for the death of babies and women in child-bed, something that was then quite frequent. The sentence of 20th September 1587 of the law-court at Dillingen states among other items: "The present malefactor, a poor female, prisoner and bound, Walpurga Hausmännin, having been accused persistently, uniformly and justly, has been interrogated gently and under torture and has now confessed her witchery and stated: Thirty-one years ago, when she had been widowed, she cut corn for Hans Schlumperger together with his former farmhand, called Bis in the parsonage. With this man she exchanged impudent words and gestures and arranged to meet him in her, Walpurga's, hut that very night and have lewd intercourse with him. Then while Walpurga was waiting for him and sat with bad carnal thoughts in her chamber, it was not the said farmhand who came to her but, in his appearance and garments, the Evil One, and they at once committed fornication. He then gave her a piece of money, which looked like a half-thaler, but which nobody wanted to take because it was bad, rather like lead... When they had finished with the fornication, she saw the goat's foot of her lover and felt that his hand was not natural but as if made of wood. This frightened her and she pronounced the name of Jesus, whereupon the Devil at once left her and disappeared.

"The next night the Evil One came again in the same guise and again committed fornication with her; he also repeatedly promised to help her in her poverty and plight and she therefore surrendered to him body and soul. Thereupon the Evil One made a scratch or a tear under her left shoulder and ordered her to use the blood flowing from it to sell herself to him. He gave her a pen to do so but as she could not write, he guided her hand...

"The above-mentioned Walpurga confessed further that she often rode out at night to various places on a hay-fork with her Evil lover, but that she could not go far because of her employment...

"She also confessed that her lover gave her a small tin containing an ointment to damage men and beasts and the dear fruit of the fields.

"He also forced her to kill young children and to do away with them before they could receive holy baptism. This she did as often as she could; she admitted as follows:

"1 and 2) About ten years ago she injured Anna Hä-

50

mannin, who lived not far from Durstigel, at her first delivery using an ointment and also otherwise so that mother and child could not be separated and died.

"3) Ten years ago the stepdaughter of Christian Walter gave birth to her first child. Walpurga gave a little squeeze to this child's little brain and it died. The Devil had particularly instructed her to kill the first born children..." There follows the enumeration of more, altogether some thirty, deaths at birth.

"She also smeared an ointment on the Governor's lady, but as she wore a necklace with some consecrated things on it, the ointment was inefficacious..."

The verdict was death by fire "after the body had been torn five times with red-hot tongs." (74)

Various means were employed in the Catholic countries to exorcize the Devil; the number of witch trials was, however, in the Protestant regions often as large as in the Catholic ones. This superstition was most widely spread in southern Germany, but witches burnings took place also in Calvinist Geneva and in Lutheran Wittenberg, and the secular authorities persecuted witches with no less fervour than did the clergy. A law of Henry VIII of England in 1541 threatened death for various kinds of witchery. The number of innocent women who were executed cannot be ascertained, as many of the protocols have been destroyed, but it has been estimated that some hundreds of thousands died as victims of this religious madness in the course of the 16th and the early 17th centuries.

Another dark chapter of the Renaissance was the wide-spread prostitution, which provided a livelihood for many women. The "wandering" prostitutes as well as the great numbers of those permanently living in the towns belonged, like the hangman, the barber, the miller, or the linen-weaver, to the group of "infamous" persons. These, however, are only a few of the large number of trades outlawed by the guild-ruled society in the 15th and 16th centuries.

The inhabitants of the so-called "open houses," supported by the towns, were looked upon as the property of the state or the community. The civic authorities protected them and the town council acted as prosecutor for them when they suffered any injustice. Compared with the middle ages, their position was somewhat bettered in the 16th century. In Nuremberg these *freie Töchter* (free daughters) were given civic rights in recompense for their services in the civic brothel and for the profits which accrued there for the finances of the town. Immigrant artisans were given free of cost the freedom of the town when they married one of them; there was no need to worry about finding substitutes for them; the economic situation, the exclusion of women from the guild controlled trades, and the dissolution of convents by the Reformation compelled many young

The Burning of Witches

girls to join a brothel. As a rule they were then excluded from civic life. A decree of Frankfort stipulated as late as in 1546 that they should be buried in the knackers' yard, and even their children had only limited personal rights and were not admitted to the guilds.

An exceptional position in this profession was occupied by some cultured courtesans in Rome and Venice, whose names were usually linked with concepts of mercenary love in the Renaissance.

Art and literature glorified the beauty of the prematurely deceased Imperia, and poets praised Tullia d'Aragona for her classic erudition and literary talents as a poet. She herself and many of her equals lived in luxurious villas, surrounded by works of art and books, wore smart and expensive garments and could not be distinguished from the ladies of society. The favour of their admirers, often of the highest rank, cardinals, ambassadors, bankers and merchants, secured their costly way of living and their exceptional position in the profession. Like the *hetaerae* of antiquity they formed the centre of a society where men in the highest positions were joined by artists and scholars, who were glad to find in the circles around the courtesans an aesthetic and cultured conversation. All the more so as the wives and daughters of the Venetian nobles lived in complete seclusion, while Rome also lacked a courtly centre dominated by a woman.

The rich wardrobe of the wealthy courtesans aroused the envy and anger of the noblewomen, who complained that their own fashions were being copied, and who demanded again and again that the regulations regarding clothes should be observed. Tullia d'Aragona enjoyed a special privilege: "In recognition of the rare knowledge of poetry and philosophy which is hers to the joy of esteemed minds," she needed not wear the stripe of yellow material on her veil which, according to a decree of the Florentine Grand Duke Cosimo I all courtesans had to wear as a sign of their profession; this veil had to cover the head, and was known as the "whores' mirror."

There were similar rules for the majority of the prostitutes, of whom great numbers were to be found in every town; they had to live in special streets or districts, and to be distinguishable by the special colours of their clothes. In Bern, for example, they had to wear green coats and red barrets, in Augsburg green stripes on their veils, but usually short yellow coats or green skirts.

In Italy prostitution reached its peak in the three decades of the High Renaissance. Eleven thousand prostitutes are reported to have lived in Venice alone at the beginning of the 16th century. There was a printed catalogue with the names and addresses and the prices of all mercenary ladies living in Venice at the end of the 16th century. When Pope Leo X decreed in 1520 that the courtesans had to leave Rome, this met with general discontent, as it was thought the town would thereby lose one of its greatest charms. It was therefore not before Pope Paul III had decreed a poll-tax for prostitutes that this profession could be somewhat restricted, having contributed so much to the fast spread of syphilis. Imported by foreign mercenaries and other armies this *Morbus Gallicus* (French illness) got hold of people of all ranks in the 16th century. Both the parents of Catherine de Médicis, the wife of the French King, died of it; the Duke of Mantua laboured for years under the evil, and many Germans visiting Italy fell ill of this plague, which then soon reached all countries. Dürer asked an Augustine father for a special prayer to guard him against this illness while he was in Venice.

North of the Alps the prostitutes, since the middle ages, had been assigned definite quarters in the towns and a clearly defined position in society. There were everywhere so-called "women's houses," and these were thought to be useful institutions, "well suited to safeguard matrimony and the virtue of maidens." Frequently married men and Jews were not allowed access; on the other hand, when guests of honour came to the town, the most beautiful inmates of the brothels were put at their disposal.

As a rule a so-called "women's host" was in charge of the house. He had to see to it that a strictly orderly life was observed, that a bath was taken every week and that on Sunday all inmates went to church, where special places were usually reserved for them. He engaged cooks and maids for the housework; often the prostitutes had to spin a certain quantity of yarn for him every day. A woman chosen by the prostitutes themselves was responsible for morals and order, and had to guard the brothel against any free competition; like the guilds, the civic prostitutes were anxious to exclude any unfair competition by "clandestine" women or by the so-called *Winkeldirnen* (pettifogger prostitutes). In 1505 the Nuremberg prostitutes were authorized by the magistrate to storm and demolish such a pettifogger house; in other towns the rival prostitutes were dragged by force from

52

their own quarters into the civic brothel. According to a contemporary report the venal ladies of Messkirch left the town in protest, "as some females have started such an impertinent and daring behaviour that the poor prostitutes in the brothel could not earn a living anymore." (33)

The mercenary armies had their own baggage train of "common women" whom the *Hurenweibel* (whores' sergeant) sometimes forced to join in the digging of trenches.

The Reformation—and in the south the Counter-Reformation—tried to restrict professional prostitution. Many brothels were closed, but, on the other hand, the brothel at Ulm, for instance, which had been closed in 1537, was re-opened in 1551 at the request of the guilds "to avoid worse disorders."

To artists the biblical parable of the Prodigal Son offered an opportunity to depict prostitutes and their background. Specializing in genre pictures of anecdotal and coarse scenes, Netherlandish painters of the 16th century, like Jan van Hemessen, chose repeatedly as the theme for their works wild drinking bouts in the company of prostitutes. "Mercenary love" was also a favourite subject for graphic work. The mercenary soldier visiting a prostitute or haggling with a procuress are well-known themes. In court circles eminent courtesans were portrayed with the upper part of their bodies nude.

Mistresses of kings and princes, who in the Baroque age often decisively influenced politics, played no equally important part in the Renaissance. The mistresses were still inferior to the legitimate ruling women, whose power was founded in their own mental capacity and energy, and could manifest itself directly, not only through the connection with a man. An exceptional place in the long line of mistresses at the French court was, however, taken up by Diane de Poitiers, often celebrated in art. She was not a courtesan, but came from the highest circles of the nobility; after the death of her husband she became the permanent mistress of the king and thus reached a position of great influence. At the age of thirty-seven she had gained the favour of the seventeen-year-old prince, later King Henry II, who had been married while still half a child to Catherine de Médicis of Florence, who was of the same age as he himself. For more than twenty years, until his early death, the young monarch gave all his passionate love to the mature woman. He showered jewels and gold upon her, gave her landed property and power and arranged for the symbolic sign of their love, the interlaced initials "H. D.," to be placed on all table plate, on arms and works of art. The four hundred thousand thaler which Francis I had bequeathed by his last will as subsidies to the Protestant German princes went to her treasury. She was entitled to dispose of the court offices and received a fixed percentage from these sales. Her magnificent castle at Anet was a second residence of France, where the clever and charming woman assembled around herself poets, artists, philosophers and soldiers, and where she ruled as a calmly calculating chancellor. In this greatly respected and influential position she was succeeded by Gabrielle d'Estrées, the mistress of King Henry IV of France.

Our study ends here with this concise survey of those women who all too often are omitted from descriptions of the Renaissance, of those who were destitute or invalids, persecuted as witches or outlawed and banished, although the large number of individual examples makes their fate even more remarkable than that of the average female population. Unusual instances among the degraded people are recorded in the reports on witches and prostitutes as frequently as elsewhere are recorded the achievements of the representatives of the upper classes in the intellectual sphere, the arts or political life. Characteristic individual destinies have therefore formed again and again the centre of our own studies, while the great majority of women—especially those of the lower orders of society—are mentioned only briefly, as the picture of their way of life could be reconstructed but imperfectly from the testimony of art and contemporary accounts.

This choice is, however, also warranted by the special character of the Renaissance: this epoch, when the importance of the individual was for the first time acknowledged, was of course best represented by its outstanding personalities. The extension of education to women, at which the Humanists aimed, was intended to free them from the limitation to family duties enforced by mediaeval feudalism and the tenets of the Church; but this could become effective only in a very restricted circle. The number of women educated according to humanist ideals was small, and only a few were enabled through their social standing fully to develop their personalities. But they breached the conventional barriers which had for centuries restricted a woman's life.

COMMENTS
ON THE PICTURES

ILLUSTRATIONS IN THE TEXT

10 *The Female Servants of Artisans, of Burghers and of Peasants*
Illustration from a pamphlet re-drawn by Antony Formschneyder, Augsburg 1540

18 *Family Lesson in Religion*
English woodcut, 16th century

20 *Visitors in the Lying-in Room*
Detail from Albrecht Dürer's *Birth of the Virgin*. Woodcut from his *Marienleben* (Life of the Virgin), c. 1501 to 1511

24 *Birth in the Delivery Chair*
Illustration from a woodcut by a master in Frankfort, 16th century

26 *Domestic Duties*
Women cleaning clothes and nursing the sick. English woodcut, 16th century; from the Roxburgh Ballads

28 *Bathing Couple in Tub*
Woodcut from a calendar from Augsburg, c. 1480

30 *In the Barber's Surgery*
Woodcut illustration by Jost Amman for the *Ständebuch* of Hans Sachs, Frankfort on Main, 1568

36 *Paula Gonzaga, Portrayed while Reading*
Italian woodcut illustration for *De pluribus claris selectisque mulieribus* by Philippus Bergomenses, published 1493

41 *The Bell-Caster*
The wife as assistant in the workshop; woodcut illustration by Jost Amman for the *Ständebuch* of Hans Sachs, Frankfort on Main, 1568

43 *Women Buying from a Hawker Displaying his Goods on a Tray*
Signed HF 1516. Illustration to Geiler of Kaisersperg by an artist in Strasbourg (Hans Frank?)

44 *Nursing*
Woodcut by Hans Weidytz the Younger, called the Petrarca Master, Augsburg 1532

51 *The Burning of Witches*
The burning of witches in the county of Rheinstein (Regenstein). Woodcut, c. 1525

PLATES

1 *Young Girl with Armillary Sphere*
Jan Gossaert, called Mabuse, 1472—1535. Wood; measurements 37×28 cm. London, National Gallery

2 a) *Lady Hunting with a Falcon*
Flemish, beginning of 16th century. Detail from a knitted tapestry. Karlsruhe, Badisches Landesmuseum

2 b) *The Wife of the Banker*
Quinten Massys. Detail from "The Banker and his Wife." Signed and dated 1514. Oil on oakwood. Paris, Musée du Louvre

3 a) *Three Peasant Women*
Pieter Brueghel the Elder, 1528/30—1569. Detail from "The Hay-Harvest" (Monthly Picture). Oil on wood; 117×161 cm. Prague, National Gallery

3 b) *Maid in the Kitchen*
From the Upper Rhine, 1489. Detail from a side-piece of an altar representing the birth of the Virgin. Karlsruhe, Badische Kunsthalle

4 *Giovanna Tornabuoni and her Companions*
Domenico Ghirlandaio, approximately 1486—1490. Detail of the fresco of the Visitation in the chapel of the Tornabuoni family, S. Maria Novella, Florence

5 *Nonnina Strozzi*
Fiorentino, 1480—1514. Medal, diameter 8.4 cm. Berlin, Staatliche Museen, Cabinet of Coins

6 *Duchess Catherine of Mecklenburg*
Lucas Cranach the Elder, signed and dated 1514. Transferred from limewood onto canvas; measurements 184×82.5 cm. Dresden, Staatliche Kunstsammlungen, Gallery of Paintings of Old Masters

7 *Elsbeth Lochmann*
Tobias Stimmer. Detail from a double portrait of the year 1564. Tempera on limewood; measurements 191 ×66.5 cm. Basle, Kunstmuseum

8 *Marietta Strozzi (?)*
Desiderio da Settignano, about 1460. Marble from Carrara; height 52.5 cm. Berlin-Dahlem, Staatliche Museen, Stiftung Preussischer Kulturbesitz, Museum of Sculptures

9 *Lady Dacre*
Hans Eworth, c. 1554/1555. Oil on wood; measurements 73.66 × 57.78 cm. Ottawa, National Gallery of Canada

10 *Old Peasant Woman*
Pieter Brueghel the Elder, 1528/30—1569. Oakwood; measurements 22 × 18 cm. Munich, Alte Pinakothek

11 *Portrait of an Old Woman*
Giorgione, c. 1506/1508. Oil on canvas; measurements 68 × 59 cm. Venice, Galleria dell' Accademia

12 *Four Naked Women (The Four Witches)*
Albrecht Dürer, signed and dated 1497. Engraving. Berlin-Dahlem, Stiftung Preussischer Kulturbesitz, Cabinet of Engravings

13 *The Seven Ages of Woman*
Hans Baldung Grien, 1484—1545. Oil on oakwood; measurements 96.5 × 74 cm. Leipzig, Museum der Bildenden Künste

14 *The Wife of Matthias Corvinus*
Workshop of Andrea del Verrocchio. Relief of marble; measurements 38 × 25 cm. Destroyed during World War II. Formerly Berlin, Staatliche Museen, Sculpture Collection

15 *Katarzyna Przybyłow*
Artist from Cracow, c. 1534. Oil on wood; measurements 89 × 132 cm. Warsaw, Muzeum Narodowe

16 *Festivity at Court with Pairs of Lovers*
Francesco del Cossa, c. 1470. Detail of the frescoes in Palazzo Schifanoia at Ferrara

17 *Pair of Lovers*
Albrecht Altdorfer, c. 1537. Fragment of the frescoes of the Kaiserbad in the bishop's residence at Ratisbon. Measurements 38 × 40 cm. Ratisbon, Städtisches Museum

18 *Room of the Abbess Katharina von Zimmern* in the Frauenmünsterabtei in Zurich. Dated 1507. Zurich, Schweizerisches Landesmuseum

19 *"Women's Bow Window"* of the New Building of the Heldburg fortress. Nickel Grohmann, c. 1562/1563

20 *The So-Called "Damenhof" (Ladies' Courtyard)* of the Fugger's House in Augsburg

21 *The Virgin with the Shivering Child*
Follower of Antonio Rossellino, c. 1460. Gilded clay-relief; measurements 81 × 61 cm. Berlin, Staatliche Museen, Sculpture Collection

22 *Saint Apollonia*
Castilian, c. 1530. Stone-pine wood; height 85 cm. Berlin-Dahlem, Staatliche Museen, Stiftung Preussischer Kulturbesitz, Sculpture Collection

23 *Infanta Isabel Clara Eugenia*
Alonso Sanche Coello, signed and dated 1579. Canvas; measurements 116 × 102 cm. Madrid, Museo del Prado

24 *Cleopatra*
Jan van Scorel, 1495—1562. Oakwood; measurements 36 × 61 cm. Amsterdam, Rijksmuseum

25 *Venus (Modelled after the Medicean Venus)*
Sandro Botticelli, c. 1478. Tempera on canvas; measurements 157 × 68 cm. Berlin-Dahlem, Stiftung Preussischer Kulturbesitz, Staatliche Museen, Gallery of Paintings

26 *The Love-Suit*
Albrecht Dürer, signed before 1495. Engraving; measurements 15.1 × 13.9 cm. Berlin-Dahlem, Stiftung Preussischer Kulturbesitz, Staatliche Museen, Cabinet of Engravings

27 *The Enamoured Old Woman and the Young Man*
Lucas Cranach the Elder, 1520/1522. Beechwood; measurements 37 × 30.5 cm. Budapest, Museum of Fine Arts

28 *A Betrothal*
Veronesian, c. 1470. Tempera on stone-pine wood; measurements 96 × 108 cm. Berlin-Dahlem, Stiftung Preussischer Kulturbesitz, Staatliche Museen, Gallery of Paintings

29 *Marsilio and his Wife*
Lorenzo Lotto, signed and dated 1523. Oil on canvas; measurements 71 × 84 cm. Madrid, Museo del Prado

30 a) *"Bride's Dish" of Majolica*
Faenza, c. 1530. Formerly Berlin, Staatliche Museen, Museum of Handicrafts

30 b) *Carved "Bride's Chest"*
Rome, 1540. Walnut wood; measurements 69 × 186 × 62 cm. Berlin, Staatliche Museen, Sculpture Collection

31 a) *"Wedding Dish"*
Nuremberg, dated 1528. Wood; diameter 43 cm. Berlin, Staatliche Museen, Museum of Handicrafts

31 b) *Lying-in Room of a noble Florentine Woman*
Masaccio, 1401—1428, poplar wood; diameter 56 cm. Berlin-Dahlem, Stiftung Preussischer Kulturbesitz, Staatliche Museen, Gallery of Paintings

31 c) *Maiden's Goblet or Bride's Goblet*
Master's mark E Z (perhaps Elias Zorn). Augsburg, c. 1590. Embossed silver, gilt. Formerly Schlossmuseum Berlin

32 *Wedding Night*
Marten van Cleve, 1527—1581. Late work of the artist. Oakwood; measurements 51 × 71 cm. Budapest, Museum of Fine Arts

33 *Betrothal of Arnolfini*
Jan van Eyck, dated 1434. Oakwood; measurements 83 × 62 cm. London, National Gallery

34 a) *Fitting in the Tailor's Workshop*

34 b) *A Cobbler's Workshop*
Two miniatures from Baltazar Behem's Codex of the town of Cracow, early sixteenth century. Cracow, Biblioteca Jagiellonska

35 *The Wedding at Cana*
Ludger Tom Ring the Younger, signed 1562. Oakwood; measurements 127 × 200 cm. Formerly Berlin, Staatliche Museen, Gallery of Paintings, destroyed in the Second World War

36 *Wedding Procession of the Adimari Family*
Florentine Master, c. 1450. Wood; detail of painting. Florence, Accademia

37 *The Bride between her Bridesmaids*
Two Women Watching the Bridal Procession
Georg Pencz, c. 1500—1550. Woodcuts; measurements 28.9 × 19.5 cm and 30.1 × 20.6 cm

38 *The Birth of the Virgin*
Master of the Pfullendorf Altar (?), c. 1500. Pinewood; measurements 102.8 × 71 cm. Stuttgart, Staatsgalerie

39 *The Birth of the Virgin*
Domenico Ghirlandaio, c. 1486—1490. Fresco. Florence, S. Maria Novella

40 *"From a Fruitful and Well-Speaking House wife"*
Hans Weidytz the Younger, called the Petrarca Master. Woodcut from *Trostspiegel* of 1530. Berlin, Museum für deutsche Geschichte

41 *The Family of Uberti de' Sacrati*
Baldassare Estense (?), 1443—1504. Tempera on canvas; measurements 112 × 90 cm. Munich, Alte Pinakothek

42 *Ladies at Needle-work*
Francesco del Cossa, 1470. Detail from the frescoes of the Palazzo Schifanoia at Ferrara

43 *Anna Codde*
Merten van Heemskerck, 1529. Wood; measurements 84.5 × 65 cm. Amsterdam, Rijksmuseum

44 *Mother Suckling her Child*
Liberale da Verona, 1451—1536. Bistre pen-drawing; measurements 21 × 27.9 cm. Vienna, Graphische Sammlung Albertina

45 *Diane de Poitiers (?)*
François Clouet, c. 1560—1570. Wood; measurements 92 × 81.5 cm. Washington, National Gallery of Art, Kress Collection

46 *Aristotle and Phyllis*
Hans Baldung Grien, signed and dated 1513. Woodcut; measurements 33 × 23.6 cm

47 *Pyramus and Thisbe*
Hans Baldung Grien, c. 1530. Limewood; measurements 93 × 67 cm. Berlin-Dahlem, Stiftung Preussischer Kulturbesitz, Staatliche Museen, Gallery of Paintings

48 *Hans Holbein's Wife and his Two Children*
Hans Holbein the Younger, 1528/1529. Varnished tempera on paper; later the group was cut out and applied onto limewood; measurements 77 × 64 cm. Basle, Oeffentliche Kunstsammlung

49 *The Artist Hans Burgkmair and his Wife Anna*
Lucas Furtenagel, signed 1527. Limewood; measurements 60 × 52 cm. Vienna, Kunsthistorisches Museum

50 *The Return of Ulysses*
Bernardino Pinturicchio, c. 1510. Fresco, originally painted for the Palazzo of Pandolfo Petrucci in Siena; now transferred to canvas; measurements 124 × 146 cm. London, National Gallery

51 *Portrait of a Woman*
Bastiano Mainardi, 1460—1513. Tempera on poplarwood, measurements 44 × 33 cm. Berlin-Dahlem, Staatliche Museen, Stiftung Preussischer Kulturbesitz, Gallery of Paintings

52 *Women Musicians*
"Master of the Female Half-Length Figures," c. 1530. Wood; measurements 40 × 33 cm. Vienna, Collection Harrach

53 *The Card Game*
Lombard Artist, first half of the 15th century. Fresco of Palazzo Borromeo, Milan

54 *Lady at a Ball Game*
Lombard Artist, first half of the 15th century. Fresco of Palazzo Borromeo, Milan

55 *The Electress Sibylle of Saxony at a Hunt*
Lucas Cranach the Elder, 1545. Detail of the "Stag and Boar's Hunt." Wood; measurements 114 × 175 cm. Madrid, Museo del Prado

56 *The Game of Cards*
Lucas van Leyden, 1494—1533. Wood; measurements 56.5 × 61 cm. Washington, National Gallery of Art, Kress Collection

57 *Cook Standing at the Kitchen Range*
Pieter Aartsen, dated 1559. Wood; measurements 172 × 82 cm. Brussels, Musée Royal

58 *The Women's Bath*
Albrecht Dürer, c. 1496. Drawing; 23.1 × 22.6 cm. Formerly in Bremen, Kunsthalle, destroyed in the Second World War

59 *Woman Cutting her Toenails*
Netherlandish-Italian, second half of 16th century. Bronze statuette; height 12.4 cm. Berlin-Dahlem, Staatliche Museen, Stiftung Preussischer Kulturbesitz, Museum of Sculptures

60 *The Rejuvenating Bath*
Lucas Cranach the Elder, dated 1546. Limewood; measurements 121 × 184 cm. Berlin-Dahlem, Stiftung Preussischer Kulturbesitz, Staatliche Museen, Gallery of Paintings

61 *Bathsheba in the Bath*
Hans Memling, c. 1485. Oakwood; measurements 191.5 ×84.6 cm. Stuttgart, Staatsgalerie

62 *Susanne and the Elders*
Jacopo Robusti called Tintoretto, c. 1560/1562. Oil on canvas; measurements 146.6 × 193.6 cm. Vienna, Kunsthistorisches Museum

63 *The Courtesans*
Vittore Carpaccio, c. 1510. Oil on wood; measurements 94×64 cm. Venice, Museo Civico Correr

64 *The Mineral Water Bath at Leuk*
Hans Bock the Elder, c. 1597. Tempera on canvas; measurements 77.5×108.5 cm. Basle, Oeffentliche Kunstsammlung

65 a) *Venetian Courtesan Wearing Breeches and Shoes on High Socles*

65 b) *Venetian Woman Bleaching her Hair*
Two engravings from Alessandro Fabri's *"Diversarum Nationum Ornatus"*

66 a) *Fan of Italian Plaited Straw with Ivory Handle*
16th century. Munich, Bayerisches Nationalmuseum

66 b) *Woman's Bag of Buckskin*
German, 16th century. Offenbach, Deutsches Ledermuseum

67 a) *Dress of Queen Mary of Hungary*
Green silk-damask with a pattern of rosettes, c. 1522. Budapest, Hungarian National Museum

67 b) *"Flohpelzchen" (Little Flea-Fur) of the Duchess Anna of Bavaria*
Hans Mielich. Miniature from the Duchess' book containing the list of her jewelry. Munich, Bayerisches Nationalmuseum

68 a) *Woman's Costume in Basle*
Hans Holbein the Younger, c. 1510. Pen-drawing with Indian ink; measurements 12.1×18.3 cm. Basle, Oeffentliche Kunstsammlung, Cabinet of Engravings

68 b) *Woman from Nuremberg in a House-dress*
Albrecht Dürer, c. 1500. Pen-drawing with watercolours; measurements 32×21.1 cm. Vienna, Graphische Sammlung Albertina

69 *Half-length Profile Portrait of a Young Girl*
Urs Graf, signed and dated 1518. Pen-drawing; measurements 23.8×20 cm. Basle, Oeffentliche Kunstsammlung, Cabinet of Engravings

70 *Dress of the Countess-Palatine Dorothea Sabine*
Upper garment of green velvet, undergarment of yellow taffeta, earlier than 1598. Munich, Bayerisches Nationalmuseum

71 *Two Women, One from Nuremberg and One from Venice*
Albrecht Dürer, c. 1494/1495. Pen-drawing; measurements 24.7×16 cm. Frankfort, Städelsches Kunstinstitut

72 *Woman Writing*
Master of the Female Half-Length Figures. Cracow, Muzeum Narodowe, Collection Czartoryski

73 *Signboard of a Schoolmaster*
Ambrosius Holbein, 1516. Tempera on wood; 50.5 ×65.5 cm. Basle, Oeffentliche Kunstsammlung

74 a) *Isabella d'Este*
Leonardo da Vinci, c. 1500. Drawing in red chalk. Paris, Louvre, Cabinet des dessins

74 b) *Courtyard of the Ducal Palace at Mantua*

75 *Isabella d'Este's Court of the Muses*
Lorenzo Costa, 1460–1535. Wood; height 27.5 cm. Paris, Louvre

76 *Anna Electress of Saxony*
Unknown Saxon Master of the 16th century (Zacharias Wehme?). Canvas, measurements 63×50 cm. Dresden, Staatliche Kunstsammlungen, Historical Museum

77 a) *Writing Desk of the Electress Anna*
Dated 1568. Ebony with ivory inlay, engraved, inside wood of Hungarian flowering ashtree; measurements 51×55×18 cm. Dresden, Staatliche Kunstsammlungen, Historical Museum

77 b) *Work Table of the Electress Anna*
Augsburg Workshop. Peartree wood dyed black with inlaid sheets of Florentine marble, measurements 145×95×82 cm. Dresden, Staatliche Kunstsammlungen, Historical Museum

78 *Elizabeth, Queen of England (The Cobham Portrait)*
Unknown Master, second half of 16th century. Wood; measurements 111.12×102.62 cm. London, National Portrait Gallery

79 *Caterina Sforza*
Lorenzo di Credi, 1459—1587. Wood. Forli, Pinacoteca

80 *Women Nursing the Sick*
Netherlandish Master, c. 1515. Wood; measurements 66.3×110 cm. Enschede, Twenthe Museum

81 *The Cure of Theodora Suarez*
Francesco del Cossa and Ercole de Roberti, 1472/1473. Detail of the predella of the Griffoni Altar. Wood; height 27.5 cm. Rome, Pinacoteca Vaticana

82 *Joseph and Potiphar's Wife*
Properzia de Rossi, 1491(?)—1530. Marble relief. Bologne, San Petronio

83 *Self-portrait while Painting*
Catharina van Hemessen, signed "Ego Caterina De/ Hemessen PINXI 1548/ETATIS SUAE/20." Varnished tempera on oakwood; measurements 31×25 cm. Basle, Oeffentliche Kunstsammlung

84 *The Gathering of Grapes*
Benozzo Gozzoli, c. 1469/1470. Detail of the frescoes of the Campo Santo in Pisa

85 *The Slaughtering of Pigs*
Hans Wertinger, c. 1470—1533. Oil on wood; measurements 33×41 cm. Nuremberg, Germanisches National-museum

86 a) *Margaret of Austria*
Conrad Meit, c. 1518. Pearwood; height 7.4 cm. Munich, Bayerisches Nationalmuseum

86 b) *Hotel de Savoye, Mechlin*
Residence of Margaret of Austria, built by Keldermann 1517/1518

87 *Woman Holding a Carnation*
Jörg Breu (?), dated 1521. Oil on wood; measurements 41×30.5 cm. Innsbruck, Tiroler Landesmuseum Ferdinandeum

88 *The Artist's Three Sisters Playing Chess*
Sofonisba Anguisciola, signed 1555. Oil on canvas; measurements 72×97 cm. Poznan, Muzeum Narodowe

89 *Peasant Woman*
Pieter Aartsen, dated 1543. Wood; measurements 95×65 cm. Lille, Museum

90 *The Milkmaid*
Lucas van Leyden, c. 1510. Engraving; measurements 15.5×11.8 cm

91 a) *Peasants in the Market*
Albrecht Dürer, signed and dated 1519. Engraving; 10.6×73 cm

91 b) *Peasant Couple Dancing*
Albrecht Dürer, signed and dated 1514. Engraving; 11.8×7.4 cm

92 *Selling from a Booth in the Market*
Detail of a miniature from Baltarzar Behem's Codex for Cracow, early 16th century. Cracow, Biblioteka Jagiellonska

93 *Fishmarket*
Joachim Beuckelaer, 1535—1574. Oakwood; measurements 127×86 cm. Cologne, Wallraf-Richartz-Museum

94 *Domestic Quarrel*
Hans Sebald Beham, 1500–1550. Coloured woodcut; measurements 36.6×25.5 cm. Gotha Schlossmuseum

95 *Peasant Women at the Harvesting of Hay, the Shearing of the Sheep, the Dressing of the Flax and on a Rustic Boating-Trip*
Monthly pictures of the luxurious calendar by Albrecht Glockendon of Nuremberg for the year 1526. Berlin-Dahlem, Stiftung Preussischer Kulturbesitz, National Library

96 *Woman Selling Red Chalk*
Pieter Brueghel the Elder, signed 1560. Detail of "Childrens' Games." Vienna, Kunsthistorisches Museum

97 *Woman Sifting Ore*
Hans Hesse, c. 1521. Detail of the "Mining Altar" at Annaberg, Annaberg in the Erzgebirge, Church of S. Anna

98 *The Woman Bear-Leader*
Pamphlet from Augsburg, early 16th century. Woodcut; measurements 24.1×30 cm. Gotha, Schlossmuseum

99 *Beggars on the Highroad*
Lucas van Leyden, signed and dated 1520. Engraving; measurements 15×18.2 cm

100 *Women Assault a Clergyman*
Lucas Cranach the Elder, c. 1537. Sketch for a pamphlet of the Reformation which was to be published as a woodcut; pen-drawing; measurements 17.9×31.4 cm. Berlin-Dahlem, Staatliche Museen, Stiftung Preussischer Kulturbesitz, Cabinet of Engravings

101 *Women Beggars*
Pieter Brueghel the Elder, signed 1559. Detail of "The Fight between Carnival and Lent." Vienna, Kunsthistorisches Museum

102 a) *An Armless Girl with a Wooden Leg*
Urs Graf, signed and dated 1514. Pen-drawing; measurements 12.3×15.8 cm. Basle, Oeffentliche Kunstsammlung, Cabinet of Engravings

102 b) *Two Women revenge themselves on a Monk*
Urs Graf. c. 1521. Pen-drawing; 25.8×20.7 cm. Basle, Oeffentliche Kunstsammlung, Cabinet of Engravings

103 *The Witches*
Hans Baldung Grien, signed and dated 1510. Woodcut; measurements 37.4×25.8 cm

104 *Woman Weighing Gold*
Jan van Hemessen, 1500—1572. Oakwood; measurements 44×31 cm. Berlin-Dahlem, Staatliche Museen, Stiftung Preussischer Kulturbesitz, Gallery of Paintings

105 *The Money-Changer and his Wife*
Marinus van Reymerswaele, signed and dated 1541. Oakwood; measurements 93.5×111 cm. Dresden, Staatliche Kunstsammlungen, Gallery of Paintings of Old Masters

106 *The Collector of Taxes*
Jan Massys, 1509—1575. Oakwood; measurements 85×115 cm. Dresden, Staatliche Kunstsammlungen, Gallery of Paintings of Old Masters

107 *Laboratory of the Grand Duke Francesco I*
Joanes Stradanus, signed and dated 1570. Florence, Palazzo Vecchio

108 *Diane de Poitiers (?)*
School of Fontainebleau, mid-sixteenth century. Tempera on wood; measurements 115×98.5 cm. Basle, Oeffentliche Kunstsammlung

109 *Welcome by the Prostitutes*
From the Middle Rhine, c. 1517. Detail from a tapestry showing a cycle of pictures of the biblical parable of the Prodigal Son; height 127 cm. Berlin-Dahlem, Staatliche Museen, Stiftung Preussischer Kulturbesitz, Sculpture Collection

110 *Young Swiss in the Room of a Prostitute*
Urs Graf, signed 1514/1516. Pen-drawing; measurements 30.9 × 21.4 cm. Frankfort on Main, Städelsches Kunstinstitut

111 *A Rowdy Party*
Jan van Hemessen, 1500—1575. Oakwood; measurements 29 × 45 cm. Berlin-Dahlem, Staatliche Museen, Stiftung Preussischer Kulturbesitz, Gallery of Paintings

112 *Female Half-Figure*
Barthel Bruyn, c. 1535/1536. Oakwood; measurements 71 × 54 cm. Nuremberg, Germanisches National-museum

BIBLIOGRAPHY

1 *Alberti, Leon Battista*, Tre libri della famiglia (ed. by F. C. Pellegrini and R. Spongano). Florence 1946

2 *Bauer, Max*, Die deutsche Frau in der Vergangenheit. Berlin 1907

3 *Beard, M. R.*, Woman as a Force in History, New York 1962

4 *Bechstein, Hans*, Reise in die Renaissance, Leipzig 1968

5 *Bloch, I.*, Die Prostitution, vol. I, Berlin 1912

6 *Boehn, Max v.*, Das Beiwerk der Mode, Munich 1928

7 *Boesch, Hans*, Kinderleben in der deutschen Vergangenheit. Monographien zur deutschen Kulturgeschichte, vol. V, Leipzig 1900

8 *Bornemann, Helga*, Frauendarstellungen zur Zeit der Renaissance in den drei Zentren: Florenz, Venedig und Nürnberg. Berlin, Institut für Kunsterziehung, Staatsexamensarbeit (typescript) 1957

9 *Brodmeier, Beate*, Die Frau im Handwerk in historischer Sicht, Münster 1963

10 *Burckhardt, Jakob*, Die Kultur der Renaissance in Italien. Collected works, vol. 3, Berlin 1955 (1st edition Basle 1860)

11 *Calojan, V. K.*, Armyanskij Renesans, Moscow, 1963

12 *Camden, Carroll*, The Elizabethan Woman, New York/London 1952

13 *Cannan, Mary A.*, Education of Woman during the Renaissance, Washington 1916

14 *Castiglione, Baldassare*, Der Hofmann (II cortegiano). Bremen 1960 (1st edition 1528)

15 *Chastel, André* and *Klein, Robert*, Die Welt des Humanismus, Europa 1480—1530, Munich 1963

16 *Chledowski, Casimir v.*, Mann und Frau der Renaissance, Munich 1912

17 *Chledowski, Casimir v.*, Der Hof von Ferrara, Berlin 1910

18 *Chledowski, Casimir v.*, Rom, Die Menschen der Renaissance, Munich 1934

19 *Danckert, Werner*, Unehrliche Leute, Die verfemten Berufe, Bern, 1963

20 *Durant, Will*, Die Renaissance. Eine Kulturgeschichte Italiens von 1304 bis 1576, Bern/Munich 1961 (2nd ed.)

21 *Durant, Will*, Das Zeitalter der Reformation. Eine Geschichte der europäischen Kultur von Wiclif bis Calvin (1300 bis 1564), Bern/Munich 1962 (2nd ed.)

22 *Eisenbart, Liselotte C.*, Kleiderordnungen der deutschen Städte zwischen 1350 und 1700, Göttingen 1962

23 *Engels, Friedrich*, Der Ursprung der Familie, des Privateigentums und des Staates (Bücherei des Marxismus-Leninismus vol. 11). Berlin 1949 (2nd ed.)

24 *Firenzuola, Agnolo*, Sopra la bellezza delle donne. Edition 1523

25 *Floerke, Hanns*, Die Moden der italienischen Renaissance, Munich 1917

26 *Floerke, Hanns*, Repräsentanten der Renaissance, Munich 1924

27 *Floerke, Hanns*, Das Weib in der Renaissance, Munich 1929

28 *Garin, E.*, L'Educazione in Europa (1400—1600), Bari 1957

29 *Gerstfeldt, O. von*, Hochzeitsfeste der Renaissance in Italien, Esslingen 1906

30 *Gleichen-Russwurm, A. v.*, Die Sonne der Renaissance. Sitten und Gebräuche der europäischen Welt 1450—1600, Stuttgart 1921

31 *Gothein, E.*, Schriften zur Kulturgeschichte der Renaissance, Reformation und Gegenreformation, 1924

32 *Gutkind, Curt Sigmar*, Frauenbriefe aus der französischen Renaissance, Leipzig 1928

33 *Hampe, Theodor*, Die fahrenden Leute in der deutschen Vergangenheit. Monographien zur deutschen Kulturgeschichte, vol. X, Leipzig 1902

34 *Havemann, Elisabeth*, Die Frau der Renaissance. Quellenhefte zum Frauenleben in der Geschichte, part 10, Hamburg 1927

35 *Hildebrandt, Hans*, Die Frau als Künstlerin, Berlin 1928

36 *Jegel, August*, Altnürnberger Hochzeitsbrauch und Eherecht, besonders bis zum Ausgang des 16. Jahrhunderts. Mitteilungen des Vereins für Geschichte der Stadt Nürnberg. Vol. 44. Nuremberg 1953, pp. 238—274

37 *Kelso, Ruth*, Doctrine for the Lady of the Renaissance. Urbana. University of Illinois Press 1956

38 *Landucci, Luca*, Ein florentinisches Tagebuch 1450—1516, Jena 1913

39 *Lauts, Jan*, Isabella d'Este, Stuttgart 1953

40 *Łempicki, Stanisław,* Renesans i humanism w Polsce, Warsaw 1952

41 *Loesch, Ilse,* So war es Sitte in der Renaissance, Leipzig 1964

42 *Lorentz, Stanisław,* Die Renaissance in Polen, Warsaw 1955

43 *Ludwig, Gustav* and *Rintelen Restello,* Spiegel und Toilette-Utensilien in Venedig zur Zeit der Renaissance, Berlin 1906

44 *Lüdecke, H.,* Lucas Cranach d. Ä., Der Künstler und seine Zeit. Berlin 1953

45 *Lühr, Dora,* Die Frau in der Kulturgeschichte des deutschen Kleinhandels. Ehrengabe des Museums für Hamburgische Geschichte zur Feier seines hundertjährigen Bestehens, Hamburg 1938, pp. 36—43

46 *Martin, A.,* Deutsches Badeleben in vergangenen Tagen. Jena 1906

47 *Martin, Alfred von,* Soziologie der Renaissance. Physiognomik und Rhythmik einer Kultur des Bürgertums, Frankfort on Main 1949

48 *Maulde La Clavière, R. de,* The Woman of the Renaissance, New York 1905

49 *Müllerheim, Robert,* Die Wochenstube in der Kunst, Stuttgart 1904

50 *Mummenhoff, Ernst,* Der Handwerker in der deutschen Vergangenheit. Monographien zur deutschen Kulturgeschichte, vol. VIII, Leipzig 1901

51 *Pandolfini, Agnolo,* Trattato del governo della famiglia (1436)

52 *Piccolomini, Alessandro,* La Raffaella ovvero De la bella creanza delle Donne (1539). Milan 1862

53 *Pirckheimer, Caritas,* Die Denkwürdigkeiten der Caritas Pirckheimer (from the years 1524—1528, ed. by Josef Pfanner), Landshut 1962

54 *Puyvelde, Leo v.,* Die Welt von Bosch und Breughel, Flämische Malerei im 16. Jahrhundert, Munich 1963

55 Die Renaissance. Berlin 1954. In: Large Soviet Encyclopaedia, series Art and Literature 22

56 *Rodocanachi, E.,* La femme italienne, Avant, pendant et après la Renaissance, sa vie mondaine et son influence sociale. Paris 1922

57 *Ruhmer, Wilhelm,* Pädagogische Theorien über Frauenbildung im Zeitalter der Renaissance, Phil. Diss. (thesis for degree in Faculty of Philosophy), Bonn 1915

58 *Scheidig, Walter,* Die Holzschnitte des Petrarca-Meisters, Berlin 1955

59 *Schmelzeisen, G. K.,* Die Rechtsstellung der Frau in der deutschen Stadtwirtschaft, Stuttgart 1935

60 *Schnack, Friedrich,* Die Welt der Arbeit in der Kunst. Stuttgart 1966

61 *Schmidt, Gertrud,* Die berufstätige Frau in der Reichsstadt Nürnberg bis zum Ende des 16. Jahrhunderts. Diss. phil. (thesis for degree in Faculty of Philosophy), Erlangen 1950

62 *Sforza, Caterina,* Experimenti. Ed. by P. D. Pasolini, Caterina Sforza vol. III, Rome 1893

63 *Sieber, Siegfried,* Die Spitzenklöppelei im Erzgebirge, Leipzig 1955

64 *Steinmetz, M.,* Deutschland von 1476—1658, Berlin 1964

65 *Steinmetz, M.,* Reformation und Bauernkrieg in der Historiographie der DDR. In: Zeitschrift für Geschichtswissenschaft, Sonderheft (Special number 1960). Berlin 1960

66 *Stricker, Käthe,* Die Frau in der Reformation. Quellenhefte zum Frauenleben in der Geschichte. No. 11, Hamburg 1927

67 *Sturmhöfel, Konrad,* Anna von Sachsen. Leipzig 1905

68 *Strozzi, Alessandra Macinghi degli,* Briefe. Ed. by Marie Herzfeld, Jena 1927

69 *Vasari, Giorgio,* Künstler der Renaissance. Lebensbeschreibungen der ausgezeichneten Maler, Bildhauer und Architekten der Renaissance. Berlin 1948

70 *Wackendorf, H.,* Die wirtschaftliche Stellung der Frau in den deutschen Städten des späteren Mittelalters. Phil. Diss. (thesis for degree in Faculty of Philosophy), Hamburg 1934

71 *Weber, M.,* Ehefrau und Mutter in der Rechtsentwicklung. Tübingen 1907

72 *Weinsberg, Hermann von,* Das Buch Weinsberg (Selected parts in one volume), Munich 1961

73 Weltgeschichte in zehn Bänden (ed. by Academy of Sciences of the USSR), vol. 3/4, Berlin 1963/64

74 *Widmoser, Eduard,* Philippine Welser, Lebensbilder aus dem bayerischen Schwaben. Munich 1953, pp. 227—245

75 *Zeeden, Ernst Walter,* Deutsche Kultur in der frühen Neuzeit. Frankfort on Main 1968

SOURCES OF
ILLUSTRATIONS

The photographs were kindly placed at our disposal by the following museums and institutions:

Amsterdam, Rijksmuseum: 24, 43
Basel, Colorphoto Hans Hinz: 7, 48, 108
Basel, Öffentliche Kunstsammlung, Kunstmuseum: 64, 73, 83
Basel, Öffentliche Kunstsammlung, Kupferstichkabinett: 68a, 69, 102
Berlin, Dr. Ernst Badstübner: 19
Berlin, Deutsche Staatsbibliothek: 95a, 95b, 95d
Berlin, Henschelverlag: 65
Berlin, Institut für Denkmalpflege, Bildstelle: 20
Berlin, Museum für Deutsche Geschichte: 40
Berlin, Staatliche Museen, Gemäldegalerie: 25, 28, 31b, 35, 47, 111
Berlin, Staatliche Museen, Kunstgewerbemuseum: 30a, 31a, 31c
Berlin, Staatliche Museen, Kupferstichkabinett: 12, 26, 46, 58, 90, 91a, 99, 103; Text Ill. 2
Berlin, Staatliche Museen, Münzkabinett: 5
Berlin, Staatliche Museen, Skulpturensammlung: 8, 14, 21, 30b, 109
Berlin-Dahlem, Stiftung Preussischer Kulturbesitz, Staatsbibliothek: 95c
Berlin-Dahlem, Stiftung Preussischer Kulturbesitz, Staatliche Museen, Gemäldegalerie: 51, 60, 104
Berlin-Dahlem, Stiftung Preussischer Kulturbesitz Staatliche Museen, Kupferstichkabinett: 100
Berlin-Dahlem, Stiftung Preussischer Kulturbesitz, Staatliche Museen, Skulpturenabteilung: 22, 59
Brussels, Musée Royal: 57
Budapest, Szépmüvészeti Múzeum: 27, 32
Budapest, Magyar Nemzeti Múzeum: 67b
Cologne, Wallraf-Richartz-Museum: 93
Dresden, Deutsche Fotothek: 77a, 97
Dresden, Staatliche Kunstsammlungen, Gemäldegalerie Alte Meister: 106

Dresden, Staatliche Kunstsammlungen, Historisches Museum: 76
Dresden, Walter Zorn: 77b
Enschede, Rijksmuseum Twenthe: 80
Florence, Fratelli Alinari: 74b, 79, 82
Florence, SCALA Istituto Fotografico Editoriale: 4, 11, 16, 36, 39, 42, 53, 54, 63, 81, 84, 107
Frankfurt/Main, Städelsches Kunstinstitut: 71, 110
Gotha, Schloßmuseum: 94, 98, Text Ill. 11
Innsbruck, Tiroler Landesmuseum Ferdinandeum: 87
Karlsruhe, Badische Kunsthalle: 3b
Karlsruhe, Badisches Landesmuseum: 2a
Kraków, Muzeum Narodowe, Czartoryski Collection: 72
Leipzig, Farbenfotografie G. Reinhold: 6, 13, 105
Leipzig, Seemann-Verlag: 2b
Lomme/Lille, Laboratoire et Studio Gérondal: 89
London, National Gallery: 1, 33, 50
London, National Portrait Gallery: 78
Madrid, Museo del Prado: 23, 29, 55
Marburg, Bildarchiv Foto Marburg: 86b
Munich, Bayerische Staatsgemäldesammlung, Alte Pinakothek: 41
Munich, Bayerisches Nationalmuseum: 66a, 67a, 70, 86a
Munich, J. Blauel, Verlag für Kunst-Diapositive: 10
Nuremberg, Germanisches Nationalmuseum: 85, 112
Offenbach, Deutsches Ledermuseum: 66b
Ottawa, The National Gallery of Canada: 9
Paris, Louvre, Cabinet des dessins: 74a
Paris, Arts Graphiques de la Cité: 75
Poznań, Muzeum Narodowe: 88
Prague, Národni galerie: 3a
Regensburg, Städtisches Museum: 17
Stuttgart, Staatsgalerie: 38, 61
Vienna, Kunsthistorisches Museum: 49
Vienna, Lichtbildwerkstätte "Alpenland": 44, 68b
Vienna, Photo Meyer: 52, 62, 96, 101
Warsaw, Biblioteka Narodowa: 34, 92
Warsaw, Muzeum Narodowe: 15
Washington, National Gallery of Art: 45, 56
Zurich, Schweizerisches Landesmuseum: 18

PLATES

I

The ladies hunting with a falcon and the patrician woman who, while turning over the leaves of a book of hours, is interested in her husband's business, are here compared with women of the lower classes: three peasant girls coming from the hay harvest with rakes on their shoulders and a maid preparing a dish in the kitchen. strong social differences are illustrated not only by actions charaistic of the persons shown but also by their clothes.

This detail from the frescoes in the chapel of the Tornabuoni family shows Giovanna Tornabuoni, the daughter of the banker, and other ladies of the Florentine patriciate in their luxurious dresses; several of these are made of brocade with patterns in the family emblems.

The obverse of the medal exhibits the profile of Nonnina Strozzi, the reverse an allegory.

Lucas Cranach painted the Duchess Catharine of Mecklenburg, a Saxon princess, wearing a beret with feathers and a dress in the bright colours popular with the German nobility in the early 16th century.

Elsbeth Lochmann, the wife of a patrician of Zurich, is portrayed in her role as a housewife with an apron and a bunch of keys; she holds, nevertheless, a pair of gloves in her hands.

The bust of the young Florentine lady is believed to be that of Mari-
teta Strozzi, the daughter of Lorenzo Strozzi who died in 1451.
Because of her beauty and her wealth, she was one of the most courted
young girls of the Florentine patriciate. Many young men applied
in vain for her hand; Bartolomeo Benci organized a magnificent
tournament in honour of the sixteen-year-old girl.

Lady Dacre, an English baroness, writing in her diary or in an account book. The portrait of her murdered husband, painted by Hans Holbein, hangs on the wall at the back of the room.

9

Pieter Brueghel the Elder made this profile sketch of a Netherlandish peasant woman as a study for a larger picture.

The simple woman from the poorest layer of the population formed an unusual model for Giorgione, the painter of the beautiful women of Venice.

Dürer's realistic study from the nude of four standing women is known as that of The Four Witches.

The ages of man, symbolizing the transience of all things on earth, was a favourite motif of Renaissance art.

13

15

Some easy-going young people enjoy themselves during a festivity at court in front of a statue from antiquity representing the Three Graces.

The frescoes of the bathroom in the bishop's palace at Ratisbon provided the artist with an opportunity to show a couple in the nude.

One of the few women's rooms of the Renaissance preserved with all its furniture is this room of the abbess of the Frauenmünsterabtei in Zurich.

The Frauenerker (Women's Bow Window) of the "New Building," in the Heldburg fortress, is decorated with figures of the virtues and other allegories, which refer to the women's apartments at the back.

The so-called Damenhof (Ladies' Courtyard) of the Fuggers' house at Augsburg, built with its arcades, about 1515, is one of the earliest German buildings completely in the style of the Early Italian Renaissance.

A Florentine patrician woman sitting with her child on a sumptuously carved chair could have been the model for this Early Renaissance relief of the Virgin.

An inscription on the reverse identifies this bust as a representation of St. Apollonia. The realistic reproduction of the contemporary fashion of the garment suggests that the sculpture may be a likeness of the donor. If so, it would be one of the very few portraits of women in Spain, apart from those in the conventional manner of court art.

The Infanta Isabel Clara Eugenia, daughter of King Philipp II, is here depicted at the age of thirteen. She wears the high-necked dress of stiff brocade characteristic of the fashion of the Spanish court at the time of the late Renaissance.

This Netherlandish painting of Cleopatra, the Sleeping Venus *has been transformed by Giorgione into a realistically depicted robust nude.*

Botticelli's slim female nude represents the Florentine ideal of beauty in the late 15th century.

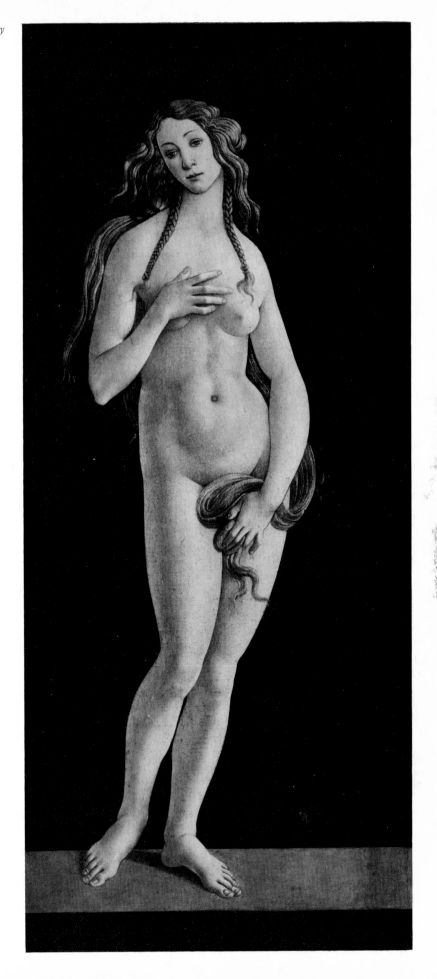

This engraving by Dürer shows an elderly man suing for the love of a young girl.

27

In this picture of a betrothal the bride is accompanied by two women; she receives the engagement ring from a young nobleman, with whom there are four friends. Although it is probably a mythological scene, it describes the costumes and the general usage at a betrothal in the patrician circles of the Early Renaissance.

Bride's dishes of majolica were popular wedding presents in Italy.

Carved or painted chests formed part of the dowry of the bride.

A wedding dish dating from the German Renaissance.

In Italy, presents were brought on the "desco da parto" to the woman in confinement. This picture of a lying-in-room shows a young man carrying one of these round plates.

Goldsmiths in Augsburg and Nuremberg made the so-called maids' or brides' goblets, double drinking vessels used for games testing the drinking skill of the guests during banquets.

On this Netherlandish painting the priest is seen blessing the matrimonial bed before the wedding night. The bride wears the bridal crown worn nearly everywhere, but shaped differently in each country or town.

On the occasion of his betrothal with Jeanne de Chenany, the Italian merchant Giovanni Arnolfini asked the Netherlandish artist Jan van Eyck for a portrait of himself and his bride in ceremonial attitudes.

32

33

Well-to-do women went to the dressmaker's workshop for the fitting of their new dresses.

The master cobbler's wife, sitting in the workshop at the distaff, looks after her child, while she is entertained by a bagpipe-playing fool. Her dress is slashed according to fashion and displays the undergarment at the sleeves.

This detail from a picture on a wooden chest exhibits a festive procession passing in front of the Baptistry of Florence. It is supposed to refer to a wedding in the Adimari family celebrated with magnificent display in the mid-fifteenth century.

Frequently the bride was escorted to the wedding by the so-called best man.

Being respectable burghers' wives, the two women watching the bridal procession wear soft narrowly pleated shawls and the usual bonnets covering the hair.

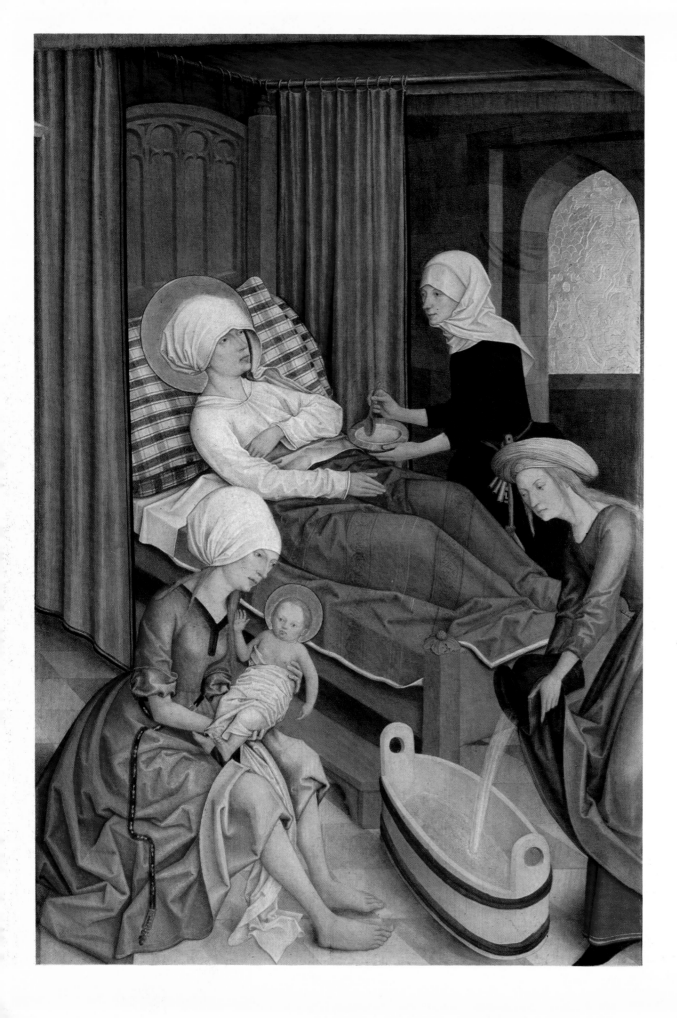

This painting of the Birth of the Virgin made by a German master around 1500 depicts the birth of a child in a rather simple burgher's home.

A procession of noble visitors enters the lying-in-room of a Florentine patrician palace. At the head walks Ludovica Tornabuoni, the daughter of the banker who commissioned this fresco for his family chapel.

NATIVITAS TVA DEI GENITRIX VIRGO GAVDIVM ANNVNTIAVIT VNIVERSO MVNDO

A family with its eight children is assembled in the spacious room of a burgher's house. The mother suckles the baby; a little girl presses herself to her father's knees, while a maid sits at the spindle supervising the other children.

In this rather formal picture of an Italian family the wife wears unusual gloves, leaving bare the tips of the fingers; this might be due to some illness. As a rule the ladies hold gloves and fashionable toilet requisites in their hands as symbols of their rank.

Anna Codde, the wife of a city chamberlain of Amsterdam, is portrayed with a spinning wheel turned in the lathe; this was a new tool at that time, at first used only in upper-class households, while the simpler women had still to content themselves with the spindle.

The mythological theme of the triumph of Minerva, the goddess of wisdom and feminine needlework was used in this fresco to show ladies-in-waiting occupied with embroidery, weaving, sewing and spinning.

These drawings by an Italian master with the motif of a mother breast-feeding her child are studies from nature.

In noble families it was customary to take a wet-nurse into the house when a child was born. The robust countrywoman, who in this picture feeds the child, is contrasted with the bathing lady and her well-cared-for white complexion.

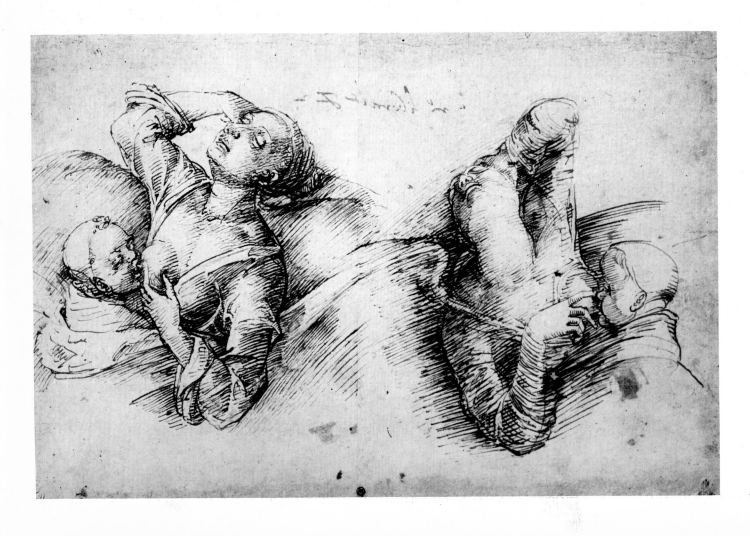

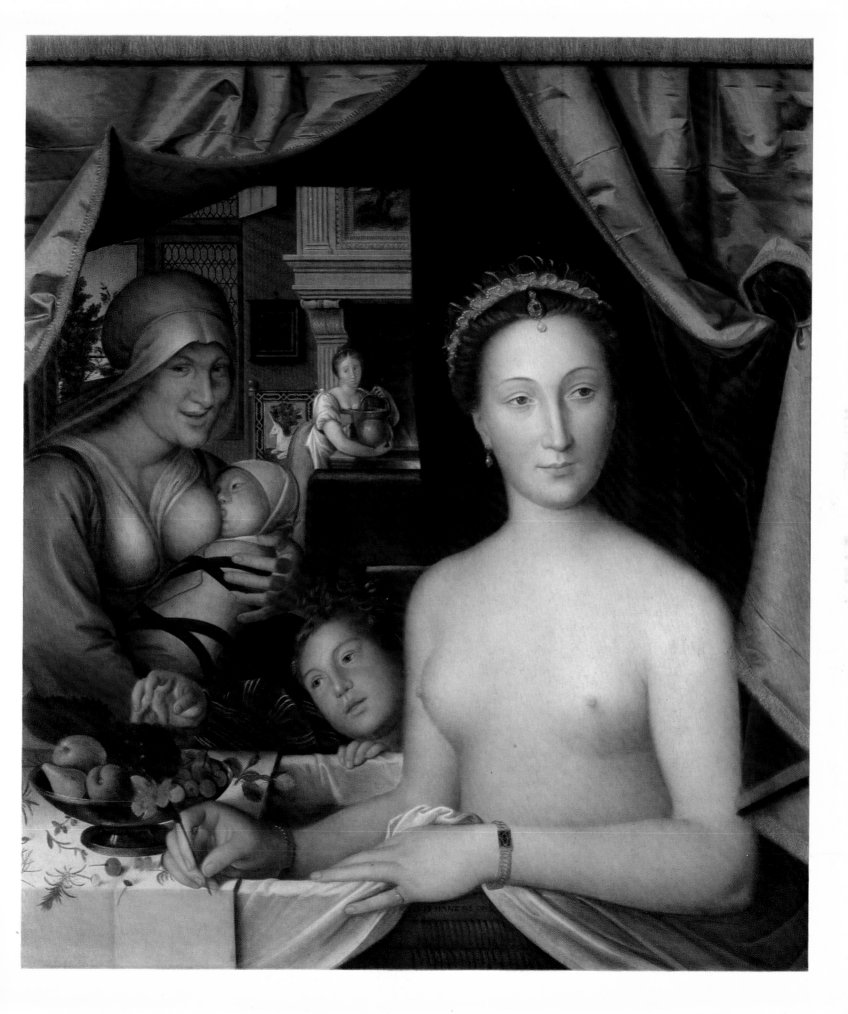

The popular Renaissance legend of the Greek philosopher Aristotle
was used as a warning against the power of women: in blind love for
Phyllis he let himself be used by her as a riding horse.

The fine characteristic representation of the mature and motherly woman with her two children and the strictly geometrical arrangement of this group of three figures distinguish the painting. It represents Hans Holbein's own family.

A scene from the Odyssey is transposed here to an Early Renaissance background; all the figures are dressed accordingly. The importunate suitors surprise the faithful Penelope, who is seen sitting at a large weaver's loom in her house; a servant sitting at her feet spools the wool. The returning Ulysses can be seen in the open door. In the Renaissance, spinning and some weaving, too, still formed part of the housewife's activities even in well-to-do Italian households.

This portrait of the wife of a Florentine banker shows clearly the use of false hair, very common at the time of the Italian Renaissance. The natural hair, evidently curled, is partly covered by a scuffia of false hair, which in its turn is decorated at the sides with curls of a slightly different colour.

51

The lute was the most popular instrument when music was made in the family circle, frequently played by its female members. Women with wind instruments were less often depicted. The music, lying open before the three lady musicians, has been recognized as the soprano part of a French song well known in the 16th century.

This detail from a North Italian cycle of frescoes shows a party of noblewomen employed in a game of cards, an entertainment to while away the time very popular in the period of the Renaissance. The ladies wear the balloon-shaped bonnets fashionable in Italy in the early 15th century.

54

The lady in the long dress is depicted at a ball game in the open air. This is probably the game called giucco della palla, *an early form of tennis popular with the noblewomen of Italy.*

Hunting was one of the entertainments of the nobility, in which women also sometimes took part. Sibylle, the wife of the Elector of Saxony, is to be seen here as an archer hunting with hounds; she is accompanied by her ladies-in-waiting.

Men and women, at card games and drinking, form one of the most popular motifs of the Netherlandish genre painting of the 16th century.

The cook working at the kitchen range is shown here in the formal image of a large individual figure.

57

Women are seen here using one of the popular public baths for thorough care of their bodies; they also wash their hair and clean the children.

This bronze statue shows a woman cutting her toe-nails. It seems likely that the motifs of the Thorn-Extractor *and of the* Bathing Venus, *taken over from the art of antiquity and very popular in the Renaissance, suggested this scene of intimate everyday life.*

Lucas Cranach gives here a realistic description of a rejuvenating bath. Old women are brought to it in carts and carriages; having taken the bath, they at once turn in youthful beauty to the enjoyment of youth and love.

The story of Bathsheba is here transferred from the Old Testament to the bathroom in a noble private house. The mistress of the house steps out of the tub which is veiled with curtains; a servant holds a bath-towel ready to wrap it around her.

The biblical theme of "Susanna and the Elders" offered an opportunity to paint dressing scenes popular in the Renaissance; here a naked woman is seen sitting with her jewellery in front of a mirror.

The two ladies in their very low cut dresses sit on the balcony of a house where the Venetian women were accustomed to bleach their hair. Both wear the coiffure fashionable in Venice in the early 16th century with curls over the forehead and a round toupee of false hair on top.

63

Leuk, a bath resort with mineral water, was at that time the most popular one in Switzerland. Men and women bathed there together in one receptacle in the open air. Passing travellers watch the people, who quite unashamedly make music and enjoy drinking in the water.

This engraving shows a Venetian woman bleaching her hair. The brim of her hat protects her face against the rays of the sun, which, on the other hand, were meant to bleach the hair to the desired golden colour.

A Venetian courtesan is depicted here wearing breeches, nowhere else recorded as a woman's clothing, though her shoes, fixed on a kind of high socles, were very popular.

Fans formed part of a woman's fashionable accessories; this one is made of plaited straw with an ivory handle.

A lady's bag of the 16th century, made of buckskin.

In the book containing a list of the jewellry of Duchess Anna of Bavaria there is a picture of a so-called Flohpelzchen *(little flea fur)*, its name pointing to the extent of the plague of vermin.

This dress of Queen Mary of Hungary is made of Florentine silk-damask, with a pattern of rosettes, the kind worn also by the ladies of the patriciate of Florence.

Hans Holbein made this drawing of a noble lady from Basle, with her feather hat, as a costume study.

Dürer also recorded in his drawings various women's costumes; this is that of a woman from Nuremberg in her housedress.

With this profile view of a young girl the Swiss artist Urs Graf exaggerated, almost caricatured, female vanity and the craze for fashion.

Dürer stresses, in this drawing, the contrast between the smarter Venetian woman in her low-necked dress and the ingenuous woman burgher of Nuremberg.

The dress of the Countess-Palatine Dorothea of Neuburg is made of green velvet and yellow taffeta.

Nec spe — nec metu *(Neither hope — nor fear)* was the motto of
Isabella d'Este.

*Isabella d'Este was equally well versed in questions of politics and
art, fashion and cosmetics, and was a leader in all of them; she
lived in Mantua as the wife of the Margrave.*

75

Because of her energy and her manifold interests Anna, Electress of Saxony, was known as one of the most eminent women of the ruling dynasties of Germany in the 16th century.

Her writing desk dating from 1568 is made of black wood and is decorated with ivory inlay.

The work-table of the Electress contains, apart from a spinet, seven compartments with writing and sewing materials, toilet utensils, barber's and apothecary's instruments, playing cards, gaming boards, etc. As there is a calendar for the year 1628 on it, one has assumed that the table was, notwithstanding its traditional name, made or rebuilt for the Electress Sibylla, 1587—1659.

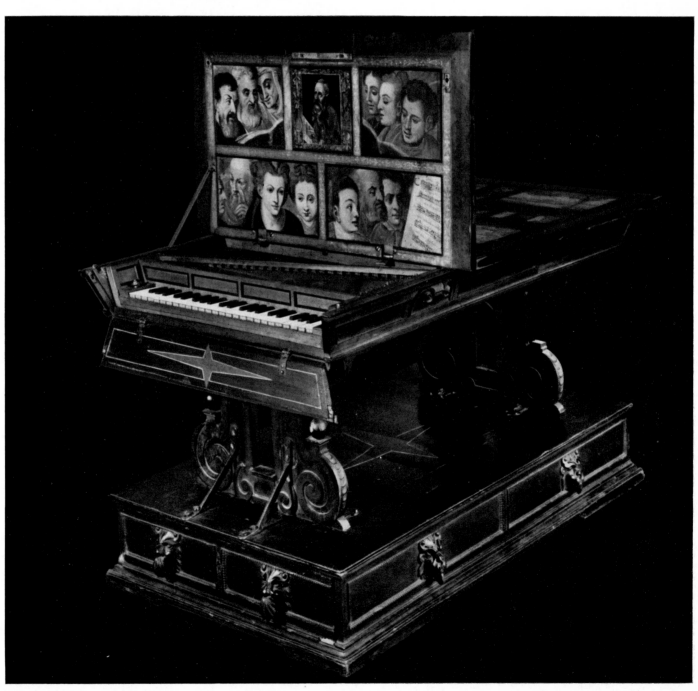

Queen Elizabeth of England, brought up according to humanistic principles and highly educated, was the foremost representative of the Renaissance in her country.

The nursing of the sick was, as a rule, the work of nuns or women in the pay of the civic authorities. This picture belongs to a Netherlandish series depicting the seven acts of mercy; it shows women working in a hospital.

This marble relief of Joseph and Potiphar's wife, in the Church of San Petronio at Bologna, is the work of Properzia de Rossi, the only woman sculptor of the Renaissance. Vasari assumed the figure of Potiphar's wife to be a self-portrait of the artist, referring to an experience of scorned love.

The Netherlandish artist Catharina van Hemessen portrayed herself while painting; proudly she put her name and age in Latin on the portrait. In the 16th century it was quite unusual to retain one's own creative work in a painting.

This detail from a fresco shows the gathering of grapes in Italy, where women helpers, too, were occupied.

85

Margaret of Austria, Stadholder of the Netherlands, commissioned her court sculptor Conrad Meit to portray her as a simple burgher's woman in a plain costume.

The stadholder, a great lover of art, moved her residence to Mechlin. Her large collection of works of art and her library were lodged there in the Hotel de Savoye, her unpretentious house.

This burgher woman wears a black dress with a white shirt set into it; the sleeves are trimmed with fur; to this she has added a plain head scarf.

Sofonisba Anguisciola, the most famous of the six artist daughters of a distinguished family in Cremona, portrayed her younger sisters in an unconventional way while playing in the garden. Chess, like other board games, served as a favourite domestic entertainment in which, as a rule, all the family took part; but women and girls also played the "royal game" among themselves.

Pieter Aartszen, the Netherlandish artist of kitchen and market scenes, painted this picture of a peasant woman selling cheese and eggs in the market. There is, however, only a slight indication of this, as her wares are rather used as part of a still life. The picture is dominated by the brilliantly characteristic portrait of the woman, whose bearing and expression show a self-confident personality moulded by work and a hard life.

Cows were usually milked by women. Lucas van Leyden's engraving
shows a milkmaid carrying a large wooden pail; she holds in her
hand a hat with a broad brim as protection against the sun.

91

A large part of the retail trade was in the hands of women. Woman hucksters, but also the wives of artisans, often sold their wares in open booths.

Especially large was the number of such women among the fishmongers. Their wives and widows, but also single women, were allowed independent activities in this trade. The picture shows a woman fishmonger standing in the market surrounded by the plentiful goods she has to sell. In the background are housewives shopping; one of them carries her purchases home on her head.

hör auff du tölpellischer tropff
   Oder ich schlag dich vmb dein kopff
Solt ich dir den hochmüt vertragn
   Woltst mein kind so jemerlich schlagn
Darumb das sie gwesen ist beym pfaff.
   Was weystu was sie hat zu schaffn
Denckstu nicht das sie hat villeycht
   Etwas vergessen nicht gebeycht
Damit hat sie vrsach genüg
   Ists wie ich sag/das sie mit füg
Wol mag gan zu München vñ Pfaffn
   Arbeit du narr was du hast zuschaffn
Vor jarn rumpelt ich auch so vmb
   Dennocht helt man mich yetz für frumm
Spey eym sein wappen rock der sag
   Das ich ein hürt sey gwesen mein tag

Losa iltis balck sehtin sag an
   Ich sach dich heut beym pfaffen stan
hieltest mit im ein engen rat
   Waist doch wie ich gestern dir verbot
Du solst der pfaffen müssig stan
   Vnd jn den weyn da heymen lan
Wenn in dir wer ein frummer müt
   Du nempst wasser vnd brod für güt
Mit mir oder ein saures bier
   Wie du wol hast versprochen mir
Zum ersten als ich zu dir kam
   Aber du redsts das ich dich nam
Jetz lauffst zun pfaffen als ich spür
   Zun büben auch zur kloster thür
Vmb bier vnd weyn du hast dein bscheit
   Dabey merckt man dein vnfrümkeit

O weh o weh du schnöder man
   Schlechst mich vñ hab dir nichts getan
Solt das vnrecht gehandlet syn
   Das ich beym pfaffen gwesen byn
Vnd im kloster beym Supriar
   Bin ich doch offt vor zehen jar
Mit meiner müter ins kloster gangn
   Wir wurden lieblich schon empfangn
Von Münch vnd pfaffen frü vnd spet
   Trügen vns zu güt weyn vnd met
Die erzwirdigen vetter frumb
   Als offt ich noch ins kloster kumb
Bring ich jn was ich jn gwasschen han
   Lest man niemand leer hin gan
Solts dann mir übelthan seyn
   Gent doch noch alte frawen dreyn.

Sixteenth-century pamphlets often depicted, in an ironic yet kindly manner, human nature as it appears in everyday happening; one such picture is this showing a domestic quarrel.

The illustrations, referring to the individual months in the calendar, show the peasant women and maids at the hay harvest, the dressing of flax and the shearing of sheep. While breaking the flax, this housewife wears a low-necked dress and a beret in the fashion of the town. In the same "luxury calendar" from Nuremberg there is also a picture of a happy outing by boat.

This detail from a picture by Pieter Brueghel the Elder shows the retail sale of red chalk by a woman. She grinds the piece of red chalk into the powder used by the artists, weighs it on small scales and sells it in cornets. Pieter Brueghel himself might well have bought his supply from a woman like this selling it in the market.

The pamphlet from Augsburg represents a woman bear-leader with
her dancing bear. She is dressed in a strikingly simple manner, decently,
like a respectable burgher woman.

Die Bern dreyberin.

Den Bern kan ich machen dantzen
Mit wunder seltzamen kremantzen
Bald ich jm den ring pring int nasen
So für ich jn mit mir all strassen
Vnd mach mit jm mein affen spil
Er müß mir dantzen wie ich wil
Ich kan jn maisterlichen treiben
Das es mir müß verschwigen bleyben
Niemandt wissen dann yederman
Wie wol ich böß nachpauren han
Die mich offt vberlaut anß schreyen
Doch kan ich mich seinnit verzeyhen
Der Berendantz mir gütlich thůt
Ich hab darbey offt gütten müt
Macht mir mein suppen fayßt vnd gůt

Der Ber spricht.

Ich armer ber wes zeich ich mich
Das ich also las dreiben mich
Ich můß mein dantz mir silber pfeiffen
Man thůt mir oft int wollen greiffen
Lupft vnd zupft mich vber tag wol
Ich müß es alles füllen vol
Die püebin vnd die cuplerin
Dar mit so get mein geltlich hin
Also gee ich vmb in der prumbs
Wen ich nuu auß dantz vnd verhumbs
Vnd worden ist mein peütel ler
Wirt ich schabab vnd gar vnmer
Vnd wirt zum dantzen nimer daugen
Den wirt mich peissen d rauch inn augen
Vnd müß darnach an klaen saugen.

Anthony Formschneyder.

This sketch for a pamphlet of the Reformation displays a band of women setting, with flails and hay forks, upon the hated priests.

Women beggars formed a part of the street scene in all towns. Emaciated women point to their children, so as to obtain alms for themselves and the crippled.

An armless girl with a wooden leg, standing in an idyllic landscape forms the grim motif of a pen drawing by Urs Graf.

In another sheet by the same master, two women are seen revenging themselves by beating up a monk, who probably has molested them.

At the Witches' Sabbath, three women are busy brewing a potion, which, according to the superstition of that time, was to injure their fellow creatures. The cruel persecutions of witches formed the reality which provided the basis for the motif of this woodcut.

The young lady uses a small pair of scales and a little box with weights to weigh the gold.

The money-changer's wife is at his side to assist him; she watches intently her husband's business. The fashionable details of their clothes prove them to be of high standing.

105

Simple country people pay their tribute to the tax collector. The contrast between the tanned face of the old woman and that of the delicate young townswoman is stressed intentionally.

There are a herb press and distilling retorts in the vault-like room. Two women are busy as helpers; they wear men's clothes, probably so as not to be recognized. The woman with the golden hair, who stands in the centre, holding a distilling retort, is thought to be the mistress and, later, wife of the Grand Duke Francesco I; she was much admired because of her lovely hair but at the same time suspected of being a poisoner. The small figure standing at the mortar might be the Grand Duke's daughter. He himself, in a fur-trimmed coat, gives instructions.

Diane de Poitiers was the mistress of King Henry II of France. She was praised by her contemporaries because of her delicate complexion. Here she is dressing herself in front of a precious mirror.

The biblical parable of the Prodigal Son provided the opportunity for depicting the atmosphere of brothels. In this detail from a series of pictures in a tapestry, the ladies of a brothel in contemporary fashionable dresses welcome their guest.

This drawing by Urs Graf shows a venal lady who receives the visit of a young mercenary soldier in her room.

A riotous scene in a tavern is represented here by the Netherlandish artist Jan van Hemessen. The women, too, are great drinkers and ready for the enjoyment of love, as is shown by the group in the background.

This half-length figure, the upper part bared, is supposed to be the portrait of Katharina Jabach of Cologne, des ertzbeschoffs und churfürsten Hans Gebhartz van Mansfeld bolschafft, *the mistress of the Archbishop-Elector Hans Gebhartz von Mansfeld.*